The Lost Temple of Israel

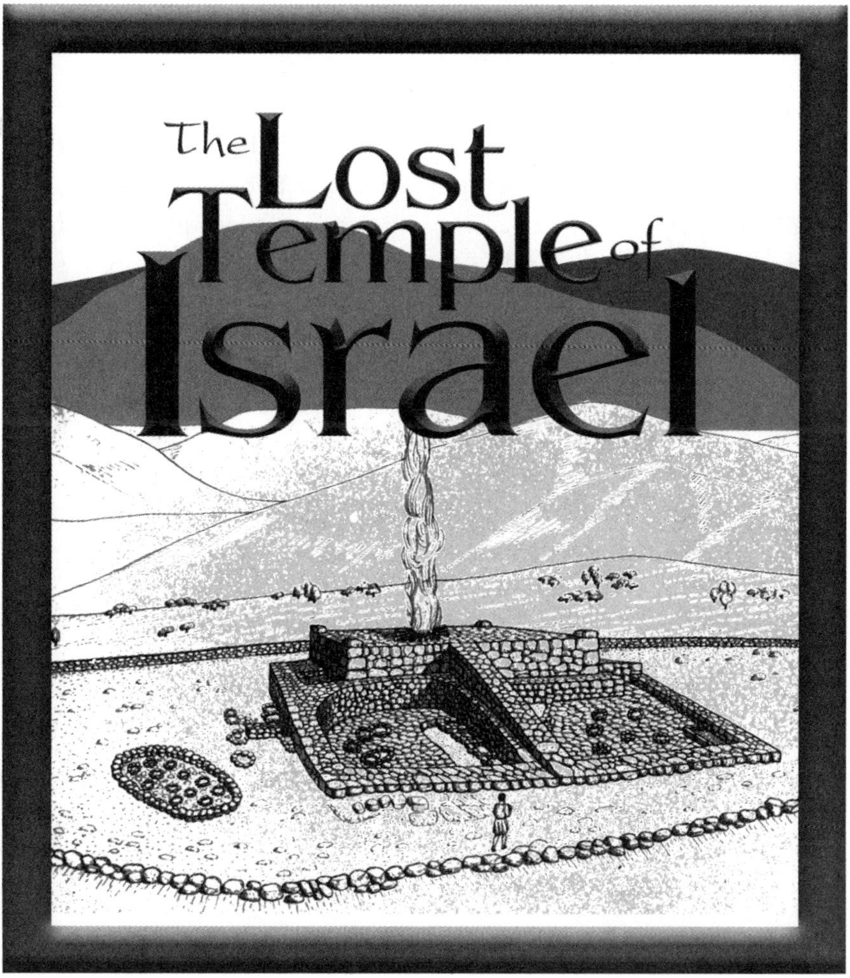

Arava Press
P.O. Box 1252
Brookline, MA 02446-1252

Copyright © 2002 by Arava Press
First printing, July, 2002
Printed in the United States of America
Library of Congress Cataloging in Publication Data

The Lost Temple of Israel:
First edition.
Edited by Elyse M. Friedman
Library of Congress Control Number: 2002093262
ISBN 0-9632793-8-6

"This day you have become
the nation of the Lord your God."
Deut. 27:9

Table of Contents

Map to The Lost Temple of Israel

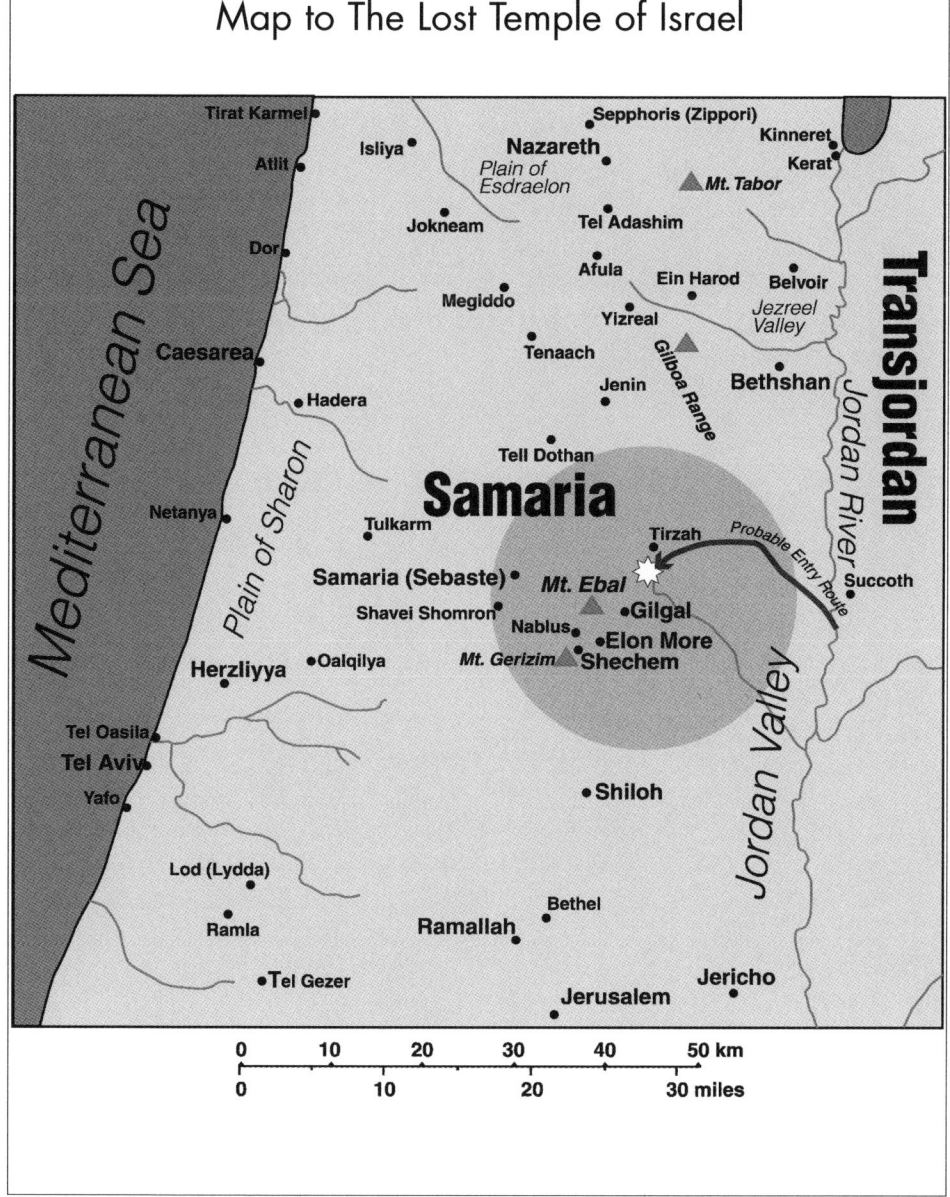

Preface

On September 11, 2001, Osama Bin Laden and his so-called religious warriors convinced me that it was time for me to finish this book and get it published.

The book, 10 years in the writing, is the result of my interpretation of archaeological discoveries made some 20 years ago; discoveries that revealed events that happened 3,300 years before that. The passage of time—10, 20, or even 3,300 years—in no way diminishes the potential impact of my story.

In 1981 a series of chance encounters led me to participate in the excavation of an archaeological site in Israel. Early on, our excavation revealed that the site had been the scene of a remarkable series of events that we could tie to specific biblical texts. Working with those biblical and other texts, I have been driven to examine related archaeological, anthropological, topological, geographical, and historical evidence. Subjecting the combined weight of that evidence to logical evaluation, I've come to what I believe is an inescapable conclusion. And I warn you that the consequences of what I have to say may very well rock your world and the world of your fathers:

The site I helped excavate is the actual site of the first Temple of the people of Israel in the land of Israel.

Contrary to universally accepted religious and scientific doctrine, the site to which I refer is not at the Temple Mount in Jerusalem. The origins of this excavation, the discoveries that emerged, and most important of all, how I put the pieces together, are the subjects of this book.

If I am right, then I submit that Jerusalem has little theological relevance. The implications of that revelation shed harsh light on the history of Western civilization. How do we understand the Crusades? A 400-year-long episode of barking up the wrong tree? Can it be that the current Israeli-Palestinian argument over Jerusalem is founded on a monumental misconception? What is the relevance of Western religion if it relies on an inaccurate memory of the First Temple of Israel?

Over the years, I have told this story to people with all levels of biblical, archaeological, and historical knowledge: from those who have no background to top experts in these fields. Once they have heard my conclusions, rather than ask for further details, most people want to dismiss them. Where, they ask me, do I get the authority to make such claims? But everyone who has had the patience to listen to the details of my research withdraws that question and subjects me to extensive interrogation. And not even the greatest experts have been able to offer reasonable alternatives to my answers.

I suggest that once you understand my conclusions, you will have to recognize the insanity of fighting religious wars over Jerusalem or—if you really think about it—religious wars of any kind over any place. Furthermore, on the basis of my findings, I feel confident asserting that no religion has a true understanding of the Bible.

*   *   *

I was most fortunate to have had the opportunity to work with the best mentor imaginable: the late Professor Benjamin Mazar. During the course of his illustrious career, Professor Mazar served as president of the Hebrew University in Jerusalem, was chairman of various departments at that university, and directed the excavations at the Western Wall in Jerusalem after the Six-Day War of 1967. I shall always cherish the generous gifts of his time and patience.

Introduction

One bright and sunny day in June 1984, a group of the world's most influential authorities in the fields of archaeology and Bible assembled for lunch in Shavei Shomron, a little town in the West Bank of Israel. My friend Adam Zertal was nervous: the experts' good opinion of his archaeological work was crucial to its acceptance in the academic community. Adam's doctorate, which focused on the survey of the geographic area allotted to the biblical tribe of Manasseh, was up for approval, and the experts' support for his conclusions about his current excavation would go a long way in advancing his academic career. Adam knew that if his ideas were accepted, it would mean rewriting many of the scientific texts that describe the earliest history of the people of Israel in the land of Israel.

The visit of those experts was important to me as well. I had worked on the excavations with Adam, but my evaluation of the findings had led me to conclusions that reached far beyond his. I felt in my bones that the repercussions of our excavations would affect not only the world of biblical and archaeological knowledge; it would also have a resounding impact on the very core of monotheistic theology, undermining some of the fundamental beliefs of Western religion.

The distinguished scholars had not traveled all the way to Israel simply to have lunch in my West Bank town. They had been in Jerusalem attending the 30th anniversary conference of the Israel Exploration Society. Professor Benjamin Mazar, the dean of Israel's biblical and archaeological scholars, had invited the group to join him on a trip to a hillside overlooking the site of the biblical city of Shechem, at the eastern edge of modern-day Nablus. They were to view the excavations that had been conducted by one of Professor Mazar's many protégés, my friend Adam. In addition to the professors, Dr. Reuben Hecht, one of Israel's wealthiest collectors of antiquities, and Hershel Shanks, the Washington, D.C. attorney who publishes the *Biblical Archaeology Review,* had come as well.

Much to my regret, circumstances prevented my accompanying the group to the excavation that day. But Nivi Markam, a friend of Adam, told me all about what happened. One scene he described is engraved in my mind. One of the most prestigious members of the delegation was Professor Lawrence Staeger, the current dean of the Harvard Institute for Semitic Studies. Upon hearing Adam's explanation, description, and interpretation of his findings, Staeger turned to Mazar, a longtime friend and colleague, and said, "If this is really what I think it is, we all have to go back to kindergarten."

In the more than 15 years that have elapsed since that day, Adam has published numerous reports about the excavations in both the scientific and the popular press. Nevertheless, the academic world has responded only sparingly, minimizing and even dismissing the significance of his findings.

It is unfortunate that since December 1987, the physical dangers imposed by the first and second intifadas, the Arab uprising in the West Bank and Gaza, have made further excavations impossible. Staeger's comment, therefore, remains an unanswered call in the wilderness. Adam's work, among the most interesting, exciting, and potentially explosive archaeological investigations of this century, has never gained significant public exposure. I am puzzled by this lack of recognition. After all, as one of the few excavations that can be compared directly to specific biblical texts, it should have generated a great deal of interest.

*   *   *

If every story must have a beginning, I believe that I must introduce my story with a brief observation about the Hebrew Bible.

Even in today's modern world, exposure to the texts of the Hebrew Bible, often referred to as the Old Testament, is inescapable. Most of us are familiar with at least a few biblical verses, whether we had religious instruction as children, paid attention in church, or even as victims of Sunday morning insomnia, subjected ourselves to the ravings of television evangelists. How much these texts have influenced our lives is very much a direct function of the extent of our individual religiousness. Perhaps no group in society is more influenced by biblical texts than the minority of Jews who adhere to the practices of Orthodox Judaism.

Although outsiders perceive Orthodox Jewry as monolithic, it is in fact a kaleidoscopic group with a range of traditions, modes of dress, and even diametrically opposing opinions on matters of religious dogma. The one factor that does unite all strains of Orthodox Judaism is the belief that the Pentateuch, the first five books of the Hebrew Bible, was divinely inspired.

Beginning with the stories of Creation, Adam and Eve, and Noah, the Bible traces the origins of Jewish history from the first Hebrew fathers, or Patriarchs, through enslavement in Egypt, the Exodus led by Moses, and the stay in the Sinai desert. The last of the five books ends with the death of Moses, when the Israelites are about to enter the Promised Land of Israel under the leadership of Joshua.

In addition to the historical narrative, the five books contain various laws and statutes that are meant to govern both secular and cultic situations. The best known of these is, of course, the Ten Commandments. Jewish tradition maintains that the correct interpretation of these laws and statutes was passed orally from Sinai through the generations, until the rabbinic sages codified them in the Mishnah and the Talmud, between 200 CE and 600 CE. The Mishnaic and Talmudic texts comprise the backbone of traditional Jewish learning.

I was raised in the world of Jewish Orthodoxy, and up until a few years ago, I believed its tenets, more or less. Let me give you an example of what I mean when I say "more or less." My study of elementary biology and geology profoundly altered my understanding of the world. I could no longer look myself in the mirror and say that, as the Bible says, the world was created in six days. As a matter of fact, few Orthodox Jews today believe the six-day concept of creation. Nor could I accept the idea that the world literally is only some 5,700 years old—the number of years between Adam and us, according to reckonings that rely on numbers supplied by the biblical narrative.

Despite these two concerns, the biblical message still has relevance to our lives. Indeed, the Talmud asserts that the Pentateuch was written in the language of people, so that everyone would be able to understand it. Millennia before Darwin posited man's evolution from apes—or worse—the first people to receive the biblical texts regarded nature from a point of view that was unencumbered by such scientific methodologies as carbon-14 dating. They had no trouble accepting the historic validity of details as they were presented in the oldest available written record, the Bible. And we today have no problem accepting that they did so. It is more difficult for many of us moderns, however, to understand how certain extreme Orthodox, even today accept unquestioningly that less than 5,700 years ago, God created the world in literally six days.

And until recently, the Catholic Church, an institution that throughout its 2,000-year history, has been less than friendly to the Jews, had also subscribed to that traditional understanding. In 1943 Pope Pius XII, who was much better informed than modern Holocaust deniers, believed that the Nazis' efforts to rid Europe of its Jews was destined to succeed. Fearing that the ancient keepers of the Old Testament tradition would soon be extinct, the pope issued an edict that called for publication of an authorized Catholic version of the Old Testament. That translation, the Saint Jerome Bible, was published finally in 1968.

Until the beginnings of secular critical biblical analysis, all Christian doctrine had asserted the divine origin of the Pentateuch. Just as the Church stifled independent, critical thought among Christians, the Jewish community excommunicated Jews who expressed disparate views. In fact, Baruch Spinoza, a Dutch Jew, brought upon himself the wrath of Amsterdam's Christian and Jewish establishments when he published his *Treatise on Religious and Political Philosophy* in 1670.

The Renaissance inspired a liberalization of thought that encouraged a more scientific and critical approach to biblical understanding. By the end of the 19th century, scholars had defined and traced several literary and historical narrative strains within the Old Testament, and especially the Pentateuch. Their interpretation showed that the Pentateuch was not the writing of a single writer—Moses—but of at least four different scribes or schools of scribes who made their contributions at different points in time. Many years later, an editor combined the writings of those scribes into one text. To this day, many biblical scholars dedicate their energies to determining more specifically who the editor and those scribes might have been and exactly when they did their work. It is important to understand that despite extensive scientific research, there is no absolute consensus. Highly respected scientists have reached a range of conclusions, emphatically disagreeing with their peers and colleagues about the correct attribution of certain biblical phrases, and indeed chapters.

I myself had been blissfully unaware of the scientific developments in biblical scholarship until 1967, when fate took me to Israel for the first time. After years of studying biblical texts within the confines of the classroom, once I was in Israel, I took advantage of golden opportunities to see the biblical texts come to life.

I find it difficult to describe the intensity of emotion I felt when I first experienced the meeting of the Book and the Land. I've noticed that even tourists who have only a passing interest in the Bible or religion discover that they rise above their apathy when they are confronted with this powerful combination. The Christian pilgrim in Jerusalem who follows the Via Dolorosa, the route Jesus followed to the Crucifixion, as well as the Jew who prays at the Western Wall, the visible remnant of the Second Temple, feel an extraordinary response that remains with them forever. Some tourists, visiting Jerusalem for the first time, are overwhelmed by extreme emotion—a recognized psychological malaise that has been dubbed the "Jerusalem Syndrome."

Although I was never in danger of succumbing to the Jerusalem Syndrome, I had an intensely strong reaction to being in Israel. As an Orthodox Jew, I had cultivated an extensive knowledge of Bible and Jewish history, and I was able almost automatically to connect the places I was seeing for the first time to the biblical texts I had been studying since the age of three.

Modern archaeology has revealed many sites mentioned in the biblical narrative, and long before I found myself in Israel, I had seen countless films and television programs that described these remarkable findings. Despite the almost magical power and sophistication of the modern media, however, they cannot evoke the emotional impact one feels when one actually stands at a biblical site. The ancient texts acquire an immediacy and intimacy that even the most gifted teachers can't hope to create in their musty classrooms.

Even the most disinterested student stops yawning when he confronts the evidence at an archaeological dig. The dusty old texts come to life when one is standing at the very location of their narratives. As always, however, a talented, inspired, and educated instructor brings the story to life. And the people who do that best of all are those who have invested years of their lives working at a particular site, sorting through the puzzles presented by its raw archaeological data.

On the basis of my experience, I can assure you that no professional actor or tour guide can match the level of excitement that is generated by an archaeologist who describes the progress of his own discoveries. Nevertheless, most Israeli archaeologists try to present a disinterested facade, discounting and dismissing emotion, which in their opinion, has no place in a scientific endeavor.

I believe, however, that archaeologists' very choice of profession refutes their ostensible dispassion. Only people with a complete sense of dedication set out to become archaeologists in Israel. Precious few achieve material success at any level. The competition is fierce, and funds for research are extremely limited. Even the most famous and most highly regarded of Israeli archaeologists endure amazing hardships to finance their work.

No Israeli archaeologist has enjoyed more renown than the late Yigael Yadin, who is best known for his excavation of Massada, which overlooks the Dead Sea. In 73 CE nearly a thousand Jewish Zealots are said to have committed mass suicide there rather than surrender to the Roman legions that besieged them.

In order to maximize each day's archaeological accomplishments before the merciless desert sun had risen high in the sky, Yadin's crew rose every morning at 3:30 a.m. to begin their strenuous work. Yadin himself consistently and diligently woke at least one hour before the rest. He used the extra hour to write a daily column for the London *Times*. Without the supplemental income those columns generated, it would have been impossible to fund the excavations.

If such a luminary as Yadin had to submit to grueling demands, imagine what unknown archaeologists encounter when they attempt to launch any kind of serious projects. Up until a very few years ago, Israel's Department of Antiquities was simply a branch of the Ministry of Education, which has been engaged in a continuous battle with the nation's pitifully underpaid teachers. As a branch of the ministry, the Department of Antiquities could expect to receive only the meager funds that remained after paying the teachers and placating people and institutions close to the minister. There was little enough left for archaeological endeavors: a bone thrown to a dog after the meat has been removed and devoured.

Since the government recreated the Department of Antiquities as an independent agency, renaming it the Antiquities Authority, its functioning has improved considerably. Still, most archaeologists find it difficult to achieve their research goals without experiencing enormous hardship. I find it amazing that despite these difficulties, the faculties of archaeology at Israel's universities continue to flourish.

Until the second week of December 1981, I was completely ignorant of the backdrop to Israel's archaeological endeavors. My archaeological experience had been limited to layman's visits to the archaeological sites that had been prepared for the public, and I'd supplemented that with voracious reading of the popular literature on the subject. But that December, I embarked on a process that thrust me into the midst of an excavation whose results and consequences would forever change my life and my view of the world.

Genesis

And this is the book of the history of Adam.
(Genesis 5:1)

In the hills of Samaria, dawn precedes sunrise by nearly an hour. It was my habit to rise just after dawn and almost mechanically put water on to boil for coffee. To make sure that the whistle didn't awaken my wife and three sons, who didn't need to get up for another couple of hours, I'd wait nearby and grab the pot just before the water reached the boiling point.

Even at 5:00 a.m., Friday, December 11, 1981, looked like it was going to be a glorious day. The early-morning sky still was studded with thousands of glittering stars. There wasn't even the hint of a cloud. I took my coffee and walked out to my tiny paved patio, which faced east. I could see the sky beginning to turn deep red as the sun started to rise from behind the mountain opposite my town, Shavei Shomron.

Most people, even Israelis, would call my town a "settlement," but I never have thought of it as anything other than a town. Located some three miles west of Nablus, it certainly does, however, fall into the category of bona fide West Bank settlements. Established in 1977 by the government of Menachem Begin, Shavei Shomron adjoins a military base that overlooks one of the most strategic junctions of Samaria: a T formation that connects the large towns of Jenin to the north, Nablus to the west, and Tulkarm, to the east. Tulkarm is only ten miles from the Mediterranean coast.

The town's original 19 families gradually had moved from their tents to small, prefabricated houses. Most of the houses, only 400 square feet, were divided into two tiny bedrooms, a miniature kitchen, a small living room, and a minuscule toilet and shower. As small as the bathroom was, it had to house the washing machine as well. Families with more than three children got an additional 100-square-foot room.

Far from luxury housing, each unit was attached to a matching twin. The paper-thin walls that separated the two units allowed people to keep tabs on one another and sustain a level of neighborly closeness without even trying. Lacking proper insulation, the houses were freezing cold in the winter, and stiflingly hot in the summer. It took a few years to get the town's narrow lanes paved, so our residents were easily recognized during the winter season. Everyone's shoes were caked with thick layers of mud.

Even that day, several years after the town's founding, the first permanent houses remained several months from completion. Later, however, when we had finally moved into the permanent housing, the fabric of our community would change, and individually we would become more self-centered. Our feelings of community would be supplanted by personal concerns. With the erosion of our sense of community, our collective resolve would weaken. No longer challenged by the demands of austerity, our brave community, like almost every other Jewish town on the West Bank, would fall prey to the social ills of self-absorption and greed. We ourselves would make it easy for our political opponents to portray us as colonialists that were imposing on the "native" Arab population of Judea and Samaria.

But on that beautiful December morning, I was feeling optimistic as I sipped my coffee and, as I did every morning, stood marveling at the scene before me. The area around our village was rich in history, and the dramatically beautiful mountains and valleys made it a stunning destination for tourists—until the disruptions of the intifada. Because I ran the administration of the town's field school, which supplied guides for tour groups, that day I would be chauffeuring an archaeologist who was conducting exploratory activities in the area. He lived just outside the West Bank.

Looking out at the mountain range opposite our town, I waited for the sun to rise. In the moments before sunrise, the sky turns a deep red, and the silhouette of a castle built by the Crusaders, appears on one of the hilltops. From the top of the castle, one can see all over Israel: Jerusalem, 50 miles to the south; Haifa on the coast, 50 miles northwest, and snow-capped Mount Hermon, at the northeast edge of the Golan Heights, more than 200 miles away. Built in the 13th century of huge stone blocks quarried from nearby hillsides, the castle's location made it easy to defend. I had visited it a number of times, and although it is empty, of course, its huge inner chambers conjure up images of King Arthur and other legendary figures.

The castle had been built on the foundations of a Byzantine church that dated back to late in the fifth or early in the sixth century. A large stone in the northwest corner of the church's foundations bears the following inscription in Greek: "From the priest Joseph, in honor of the prophet Elijah."

What does Elijah have to do with that particular hilltop? The answer is in II Kings 1. The Bible tells the story of Ahazia, king of the Northern Kingdom of Israel. His great-grandfather, Omri, founded what was then the kingdom's capital city, Shomron, and that city had expanded under the rule of Ahazia's grandfather, Ahab, husband of the infamous Jezebel. Like most rulers over Israel, Ahazia had resisted the religion of the Israelites, preferring the idol worship of the Canaanites. Falling ill and eager to learn his fate, the king sent messengers to seek out a priest of Beelzebub, an idol god. On their way to find the priest, the messengers encountered Elijah, who questioned them about their mission. Hearing their answer, he sent them back to their king, instructing them to tell him that rather than worshipping idols, he should turn to the God of Israel.

Furious with Elijah, the king sent out a company of 50 soldiers to arrest him and bring him back to Shomron to stand trial. But when Elijah saw the soldiers coming for him, he cried out to God, and the soldiers were broiled to a crisp by fire from heaven. A second group of soldiers met the same fate.

The captain of the third group of royal soldiers was more practical. He himself approached Elijah, leaving his men behind. Ahazia's captain appealed to the prophet, asking that he not harm the soldiers, who were doing nothing more than their duty to their king. Elijah told him to return to the king and tell him that because of his failure to believe in the God of Israel, he would die. And that, according to the Bible, is what happened.

As I reflected on that story, my gaze shifted north of the castle to the hill that contains the remains of the ancient city of Shomron. In Arabic, the hill with the castle is called Sheikh Sha'ali, or hill of the flame. That flame is, of course, the biblical flame that consumed Ahazia's soldiers. Both Moslem and Christian traditions, therefore, draw a connection between this hill and Elijah, one of the greatest prophets of Israel. Elijah, Jewish tradition holds, will herald the coming of the Messiah.

I finished my coffee, rinsed out my cup, and went to get the school's Peugeot van. I drove west toward the Mediterranean coast as the sun was rising behind me. The natural beauty of Samaria revealed itself in shades of brilliant green, soft browns, and the extravagant colors of the wild flowers that grow everywhere at that time of year.

The road to the coast follows a brook known as Nahal Shechem. Although like most of Israel's waterways, it is thoroughly polluted by industrial wastes, that day under the winter sun, Nahal Shechem looked bright, clear, and clean. Noting the fig, almond, lemon, and ubiquitous olive trees that grow alongside the road, I reminded myself that at the end of January, just a few weeks later, the pink and white blossoms of the almond trees would burst forth, and it would be time to plant new trees.

I had driven about half an hour, when I arrived at the gates of Kibbutz Ein Shemer. Like most kibbutzim that were politically opposed to the Begin government, especially to settlement of the West Bank, Kibbutz Ein Shemer, a member of the left-wing Hashomer Hatzair party, was diametrically opposed to groups like mine that had moved into the West Bank.

The philosophy of Hashomer Hatzair is secular, founded on socialist principles. Its members make a point of publicly expressing disdain for Jewish religious traditions, and they have made sure to keep their educational system completely free of anything even remotely religious. Wearing a yarmulke that marked me as an observant Jew, as I drove through the gates of the kibbutz, I thought to myself, "I bet the Catholic kids I knew when I was growing up in New York City know more about Judaism than any kid who has grown up here."

To Hashomer Hatzair, Jewish holidays are celebrations of the annual agricultural cycle, not that different from the festivals of the ancient Canaanites. Not until the age of 18 or 19, when they are serving in Israel's armed forces, do the youths of Hashomer Hatzair experience any kind of traditional Judaism. In the army, all segments of Israeli society meet: secular, traditional, and even quite observant Orthodox Jews.

Hashomer Hatzair viewed the promise of Zionism in socialist egalitarianism, which along with other nationalist movements arose at the tumultuous end of the

19th and beginning of the 20th centuries. Its connections with traditional Judaism were tenuous, at best.

When Zionism was young, the socialist kibbutzim were instrumental in the creation of the State of Israel. I have no doubt that it was the dedication and sacrifice of the kibbutzniks that ensured the formation of our Jewish homeland. Up until recent years, their sons were disproportionately represented in the elite military units, and a brief walk through any kibbutz cemetery will attest to their sacrifices.

Reading the inscriptions on their tombstones, one can begin to understand and appreciate the struggles of the early kibbutzniks: not only did many of them lose their lives fighting an enemy who objected to their regaining the land after 2,000 years in exile, many of them died of malaria and other diseases because they were situated so far from adequate medical resources.

During the period of the British Mandate, which preceded Israeli independence in 1948, the kibbutzim were instrumental in protecting and hiding Jewish refugees who had managed to get through the British blockades and disembark undetected on the Mediterranean beaches. Kibbutzniks also helped camouflage the activities of the Haganah underground, and they formed the backbone of the Palmach units that fought bravely during the War of Independence.

In recent years, however, the socialist force that fueled the kibbutz movement has been disintegrating rapidly. With agriculture no longer being the major source of their income, the kibbutzim have turned to manufacturing. The new structures of industrialism don't support true equality among kibbutz members, and members who are trained to assume the more responsible industrial jobs are becoming the elite of kibbutz society. The pure socialism of the founding fathers has dissipated into a series of compromises, and today's kibbutzim are operating under what looks like some kind of collective capitalism. Financially stricken these days, almost every kibbutz is currently in receivership. Although I considered the utopian socialist attitude of the kibbutzniks to be unrealistic, I had always admired their good intentions.

As a religious member of a West Bank settlement town, I had had few encounters with Hashomer Hatzair kibbutz members, so I was curious about the man I'd be driving that day. It was 5:30 a.m. when I entered the kibbutz dining room, an enormous glassed-in room that could seat 800 people comfortably. The rising sun lit the room, and I spotted a single man sitting at a table, silently sipping coffee. I walked toward him, and as I drew nearer to him, he greeted me with a friendly smile. "Shalom," he said, "I'm Adam."

"Shalom, I'm Zvi," I responded, shaking his outstretched hand.

He motioned toward the coffee urn, and after a moment's pause, I stepped forward and poured myself a cup. My hesitation was due, of course, to my lifelong strict adherence to the laws of kashrut, or keeping kosher. Orthodox Jews won't eat or drink anything prepared in Hashomer Hatzair kibbutzim, which reject the laws of kashrut completely and unequivocally. I knew, however, that because the coffee had been made in a machine that was used only for brewing coffee, it was OK. I drank it from a clear glass cup, so I was complying with the most stringent Orthodox practices. As it turned out, that cup of coffee was to be the first of oceans of coffee the two of us would drink together over the years of our subsequent friendship. I sat down with my coffee, and we discussed the plan for the day. Adam would be lecturing at our field school and leading a tour of areas that he had surveyed as part of his archaeological research.

My first impression of Adam was certainly influenced by his easy, warm smile and sparkling brown eyes. I noticed a pair of crutches leaning against a chair next to Adam, but it didn't seem possible that they could be his. I could tell that Adam was about my height, six feet tall, but his shoulders were much broader than mine. His round, full-cheeked face was framed by short, curling, dark brown hair that was just starting to recede. And his thick neck looked right for a dairy farmer who spent at least some of his time milking the cows in the kibbutz's modern dairy farm.

So long as he was seated, I wondered whether the crutches were actually his, and if they were, how he had come to need them. In Israel, so many people have been crippled in the sequence of wars and attacks that have always plagued the country. Also, the country has some of the worst road-safety statistics in the world.

When later we had become friends, Adam told me that he had been wounded in one of Israel's wars. In October 1973 Adam was commander of a platoon in the Israeli Engineering Corps. He had led his unit as part of the Yom Kippur War forces that crossed the Suez Canal, encircling and besieging the Egyptian Third Army. This maneuver, brilliantly conducted by General Ariel Sharon, may very well have been the turning point in the war, leading to a cease-fire.

Adam's legs had been wounded while he was crossing the canal, and he was hit again when his party landed on its west bank. As a result of those injuries, Adam had spent nearly a full year recuperating in a hospital. I didn't realize just how severe his wounds had been until spring arrived and I saw him wearing shorts. His legs are heavily pockmarked with the imprints of bullets and shrapnel.

Israel's Ministry of Defense spends a fortune on and devotes extensive effort to the rehabilitation of wounded soldiers. The casualties of the Yom Kippur War included a large number of psychological trauma victims. I am sure every war affects the psyches of its soldiers in much the same way. Israelis, living among so many wounded veterans, are keenly aware of the problem, which grows increasingly painful with each successive war.

During Adam's hospital convalescence, his bed was next to the bed of another wounded soldier, Yoram Zafrir, an archaeologist. Adam had been trained as an economist, specializing in agriculture. But he had always had a strong interest in archaeology. When they were teenagers, Adam and his friend Nivi Markam had volunteered and participated in Yigael Yadin's excavation of Massada, overlooking the Dead Sea. And throughout their youth, the two boys had regularly spent hours walking around the vicinity of their kibbutz, examining the numerous archaeological sites and gathering interesting pottery shards.

His hospital friendship with Zafrir prodded Adam to pursue a formal study of archaeology at the Hebrew University in Jerusalem. Because at first he was unable to attend lectures, instructors and professors came to the hospital and gave him private bedside instruction.

Adam completed the requirements for his bachelor's degree in 1977, at the relatively advanced age of 33, and immediately he began to work on his master's degree. The subject of his thesis, which he later expanded into a doctoral dissertation, was an archaeological survey of the geographic area allotted to the biblical tribe of Manasseh, one of the sons of Joseph. The area covered in Adam's dissertation survey is entirely within the bounds of the West Bank, and except for a sprinkling of Jewish towns, it is populated almost exclusively by Moslem Arabs.

That region, detailed in the Book of Joshua (17:1-11), comprises much of what is today called Samaria. Although television news programs are forever splashing the map of Israel on TV screens worldwide, their reporters consistently fail to describe the complex differences between Samaria and the areas that border it.

Near Adam's kibbutz, numerous exclusively Arab towns in the area called Wadi Ar'a have been part of Israel since 1948, much to the regret of the mostly Moslem population. The northwest corner of Samaria is just south of Wadi Ar'a. Samaria and Judea had been annexed by Jordan after Israel's War of Independence, but England and Pakistan were the only governments that recognized Jordan's annexation. The borders that were created following the cease-fire in 1949 were drawn so arbitrarily that a number of those Arab towns were split down the middle—one side going to Israel, the other to Jordan.

In such situations, the town on the Israeli side, although it never got as much government funding as a Jewish town, was always much more sophisticated and better developed than its Jordanian counterpart. The Israeli side of these towns enjoyed much better educational systems, postal service, sanitation, and road maintenance than the side controlled by Jordan.

The Israeli Arabs from those towns that had been part of Israel since 1949 had grown to know Israel, which, although it is far from perfect, remains a democratic state with deeply rooted humanitarian commitments. Undoubtedly, most Israeli Arabs would have preferred being ruled by other Arabs, but they have learned about the democratic nature of Israeli society. The Arabs of the West Bank and Gaza, which Israel captured in 1967, don't share the understanding that their Israeli brethren have developed over the more than 50 years since Israeli independence.

Like other Arab countries, Jordan and Egypt have an iron grip on the mass media, which always present Israelis in an extraordinarily fiendish light. I was shocked by the textbooks used by the Arab children in the schools of Gaza and the West Bank. I saw the books in Tel Aviv in 1968, when they were on display at an exhibit following the end of the Six-Day War. Even the Nazi propaganda minister, Joseph Goebbels, never taught the principles of first-grade arithmetic by asking,

"How many dead Jews do you get if you kill three Jews one day and four Jews the next?" But in Egyptian-controlled Gaza, that's the sort of "problem" first graders were asked to solve.

Having been subject to extreme hatemongers for so many years, it was no wonder that the Arabs of the West Bank and Gaza were astonished that the conquering Israelis did not slaughter them at will in 1967. Their initial shock took 20 years to wear off. Then, in December 1987, the spark of the intifada would fire up active rebellion against the Israelis.

Up until 1987, in the eyes of the Arabs of the West Bank and Gaza, Israel was only one in a series of conquerors—Ottoman Turkey, England, and Jordan, not to mention the various Arab rulers—who had controlled the land of Israel since the armies of Mohammed had swept across the Middle East in 640. There has never been "self-rule" by local Arabs in the land of Israel.

As Adam and I were driving to Shavei Shomron to pick up our guides, I asked him about his survey. He told me that when he first embarked on the survey, he had found that the local Arabs responded with deference and even helpfulness. Despite occasional outbursts of hostility, he and his crew felt comfortable roaming freely throughout the fields and mountains of Samaria. They conducted interviews and conversations with many of the local Arabs, especially the elders, whose memories were treasure troves of critical information and invaluable folklore related to the various sites.

Adam's goal was to document every single archaeological site within the survey's area, which covered more than 2,000 square kilometers. Progress on the survey, which Adam had nearly completed, has been hindered since the beginning of the first intifada in 1987. Since then, travel in open jeeps around Arab towns has been a risky undertaking.

One might wonder how it could be possible for Israel's arid terrain to support the societies that left behind the artifacts of their lives. In addition to its paucity of water, the land of Israel lacked the extensive mineral deposits that would have attracted large populations for mining. Furthermore, perennially caught between major powers both north and south, Israel was the site of many wars, and it was crisscrossed by trade routes reaching from border to border. Even with those mitigating circumstances, Israel is home to a staggeringly high number of ancient sites. Perhaps this richness of history attests to her eternal attraction. And the struggle to gain control of this tiny, unique land continues with no sign that it will end anytime soon.

Large armies found the coastal road alongside the Mediterranean Sea a most hospitable route, and the Romans dubbed it Via Maris, or the "sea route". With the foreign armies controlling the coast, the indigenous populations found the hilly areas of central Israel to be the safest places to establish their towns. And the greatest settlement did indeed occur in the mountainous regions of central Israel that stretch from the northern edge of Samaria, south past Jerusalem, and extend beyond the hills of Hebron that meet the southern Negev plain just north of Beersheba. By contrast, the population of modern Israel is concentrated along the coast.

As we drove toward Shavei Shomron, Adam explained that the first really intensive survey of this area had been conducted soon after the Six-Day War of 1967, when Israel captured the West Bank and Gaza. Even then, the fate of the captured territories was uncertain, and the Department of Antiquities was eager to expedite exploration of that area that was so rich in ancient history. About 200 sites had been identified within the area that Adam would later survey, and many of those had been identified earlier in more primitive surveys that had been undertaken late in the 19th and early in the 20th centuries.

In his own survey of Manasseh, Adam told me, he and his crews had already registered more than 2,000 sites in the same area. What is the reason for the remarkable difference in the number of identified sites? The earlier survey had confined its investigations to a narrow time frame by checking out only those sites that were accessible from the main thoroughfares. Adam and his crew, however, followed a much more intensive methodology: they examined every meter of the area, hill by hill, valley by valley.

The approach Adam created and which eventually he computerized, examined every site according to some 30 distinct criteria that included size, agricultural produce, access to water, visibility, and access to thoroughfares.

What does it take to identify an ancient site? It is extremely rare that one stumbles across remnants of ancient structures on the surface. Aside from deterioration caused by exposure to nature, the many wars over the centuries served to destroy the great majority of ancient buildings. In the entire country, only a few dozen such structures remain visible today.

The factor that definitively identifies an ancient site is a concentration of pottery. In antiquity, pottery was relatively easy to make and, like today, even easier to break. At one time almost all cooking and storage utensils were made of pottery. Metal came into common use only in the most recent millennium. With increasingly accurate methods for dating pottery shards, scientists' identification of archaeological sites is getting more precise.

How does a survey team determine whether a particular area might prove archaeologically interesting? The team members scan the area for the heavy concentrations of pottery that signal bygone inhabitation. In rare instances, they find other items, such as flint knives, pieces of glass, and even coins.

In the last 50 years, the ability to date certain types of pottery with great accuracy has developed by leaps and bounds. For example, following the Six-Day War, Israeli archaeologists finally had access to the Western Wall of the Temple in Jerusalem. Because it is well established that the wall's builder, King Herod, reigned from 37 BCE to 4 BCE, the pottery that was unearthed there could be identified as having been produced during this narrow time span. Most of the pottery that was found above the wall was from a later period, and the pottery that was buried lower was from an earlier period. The system of identifying deepest finds as having originated in the earliest periods and those found closest to the surface as being from later periods is one aspect of what is known as stratigraphy. This description of excavating a *tel*, or "ancient mound," such as the tel James Michener popularized in his novel *The Source,* is certainly oversimplified. Not all peoples built on the ruins of a prior era. Some completely removed all debris so that they could build from the bedrock up.

Until recently, most archaeological investigations focused on the expensive and time-consuming excavation of tels. But with their improved ability to identify ancient pottery, scientists have in the last 30 years, redirected their energies, and increasing numbers of them are conducting surveys. Pottery dating is becoming dramatically more precise, and the origins of certain shards have been pinpointed to within a specific 20- or 30-year period of time. The investigators classify the groups of pottery unearthed at each site, allowing them to map the area to show where, when, and how people lived within its boundaries. Adam explained that he calls the kind of research he does, "width stratigraphy."

The hour Adam and I spent together that morning was the beginning of my education in archaeology. It was the first of what grew to be thousands of hours I would spend talking with him and other archaeologists, reading textbooks, and engaging in serious visits to Israel's museums, especially the Israel Museum and the Rockefeller Museum in Jerusalem.

From that first morning, I found myself captivated by Adam and his enthusiasm for his work. And later, when I was able to understand the demanding nature of his work, which required him to spend at least one day of every week walking over extremely rough terrain, I was amazed that he, a man who walked with crutches, was able to do so much. When I met him, he had already completed four years of the survey.

As the years went by, Adam improved his ability to walk by engaging in physical therapy and a steady regimen of swimming. When we first met, he generally depended on two crutches. These days, he rarely uses even one. He told me that he had set his sights on performing the survey with the knowledge that to succeed, he would need to overcome his physical handicap. And he viewed the survey as an integral part of his physical, emotional, and psychological recuperation.

Even that first day, as he described his project, Adam was able to sense my enthusiasm for his work, and eventually he allowed me to become part of his "inner circle." I became a regular within days. Our group of devotees, coming from different walks of life, share most of all a great admiration for and friendship with Adam. In addition, we all have a great love for the land and history of Israel. And we consider Adam's work worthy of any support we can offer.

Nivi Markam who, like Adam, hails from Kibbutz Ein Shemer, was always the most important member of this exclusive club. A lifelong friend of Adam, Nivi is soft-spoken, sensitive, and mild-mannered. Fortunately, the kibbutz had allowed him to accompany Adam on the survey and other projects. Nivi's mechanical genius kept Adam's dilapidated jeep in working order. More than once, I watched him use string from his pocket to perform an emergency repair and save us from being marooned in the most perilous areas of the West Bank.

In his trademark black felt hat that looks like a hand-me-down from Indiana Jones, Nivi was the practical administrator who balanced Adam's more theoretical enthusiasms. Nivi could always be relied upon to come up with efficient and economical solutions to solve problems that most people would solve by throwing a lot of money at them.

When he wasn't helping Adam, Nivi worked in the kibbutz's zoo, its nursery, the avocado fields, and at any other tasks to which he might be assigned. I cannot remember hearing him complain; he accepted even the most difficult situations with serenity.

In addition to Nivi, Adam usually needed at least one more person to do the work. No more than six of us could squeeze into Adam's jeep, so we all became good friends. Other commitments kept some of us from regularly participating in the survey, which, like Adam's and my first meeting, generally began very early on Friday mornings and ended at dark. Despite the demands, there was a dependable group of enthusiasts who kept the survey manned without interruption throughout the years.

With Nivi in the driver's seat, the rest of us would pile into Adam's jeep and leave the kibbutz at about 5:00 a.m., heading for the area that Adam had designated for the survey. Once we'd arrived at the site, Nivi would park the jeep on a hillside so that we'd be able to see it no matter where we were working.

Adam then would set each of us on a parallel course, 10 to 20 meters apart, and we would begin walking. Aiming above all not to offend the local populations, each of us took meticulous care not to damage any plants or trees, but because most of the ancient sites are on uncultivated hilltops, such care was generally unnecessary.

The trick, I found out the first day I participated, is to be able to distinguish pottery shards from the pebbles, rocks, green overgrowth of weeds and flowers, and different shades of soil. The sites we explored were varied according to the seasons of the year. From January through June, the rainier half of the year, so much shrubbery grows that the pottery shards are well hidden beneath the green carpet of flora that cover every unpaved inch of ground. During those months, we concentrated on the fringe areas of eastern Samaria, east of the watershed. In that region, the average annual rainfall is less than 150 millimeters, compared with the 600 millimeters that fall on the western side of the watershed. With no natural ground cover, those areas much more readily exposed their pottery pieces to us.

From July through December, when most of the greenery wilts for lack of rain, we devoted our energies to the more heavily cultivated and populated areas west of the watershed.

In my early days as an "archaeologist," I was quite confident that every piece of pottery I found was going to be a major contribution to science. It took me a while to realize that only those pieces that can be associated with a particular kind of jar or pot are of value. Such indicative pieces bear a noticeable sign—a handle or part of a handle, the lip of a pot, a stripe, or a particular design. When such fragments are presented in the professional literature, they are drawn in black as part of the imagined whole, and the undiscovered parts of the vessel are depicted in white, with a black outline.

Whenever one of us found an interesting object or shard, everyone would gather for an ad hoc conclave to analyze and categorize the piece. A wide, childlike grin from Adam was the sign that we had unearthed a piece that seemed to have real significance. As the weeks progressed, I developed a knack for identifying pottery shards from afar—even those that were well camouflaged against the soil, rocks, and green shrubbery.

Each morning we'd spend three hours combing our designated areas before convening for breakfast. Everyone brought something from home, and in addition to the treats Nivi rustled up from the kibbutz—olives, hard-boiled eggs, vegetables, and bread—we looked forward to the special tea Nivi would brew for us. Even in the most desolate areas, he was able to find and identify weeds that were suitable for tea. As we sat under a tree, sipping our freshly brewed tea, our conversations ranged from our own work to current events, national politics, the politics of the academic archaeological world, and inevitably, the difficulties of funding the research.

In Israel, arguing about politics is a national pastime, but although our opinions ranged from far right to far left, we rarely raised our voices. Each of us realized that nothing one of us might say would convince any of the others to mend his ways. Certainly the political opinions of Hashomer Hatzair kibbutzniks would be wildly different from mine. My town, Shavei Shomron, was established by the movement known as Gush Emunim.

The Gush Emunim movement traces its origins to the teachings of Rabbi Avraham Kook, who during the time of the British Mandate was the first Chief Rabbi of Israel. Rabbi Kook interpreted the historical appearance of the Zionist movement as the beginning of redemption, or the messianic era. His disciples, particularly his son Rabbi Zvi Yehuda Kook, interpreted Israel's capture of the biblically rich West Bank in the Six-Day War as a critical step that heralded the coming of the messiah.

Gush Emunim, led by former students of Yeshivat Merkaz Harav, named after the first Rabbi Kook, started to emerge in the late 1960s and early 1970s, gradually evolving as a religious, right-wing splinter group of the larger, Movement for a Greater Israel, *Tnu'a Lema'an Eretz Yisrael Hashleyma,* which formed after the Six-Day War and whose broad membership included both religious and nonreligious Jews. The goal of Movement for a Greater Israel was the complete annexation of the Golan Heights, the West Bank, and Gaza.

Many members of Movement for a Greater Israel were from collective farms and kibbutzim that had been associated with the Labor Party, and one of its staunchest supporters was Yitzhak Tabenkin, who, like Yitzhak Rabin, had been among the leading members of the Achdut Avoda kibbutz group. Members of Movement for a Greater Israel believed that security concerns justified annexation: Israel should never yield the ranges of mountains that overlook its highly populated Mediterranean coastal region.

Members of Movement for a Greater Israel were instrumental in establishing towns and kibbutzim in the Golan Heights, which Israel had captured from Syria in 1967. There was broad consensus in Israel, and there probably still is, for keeping that territory. Throughout the first 19 years of Israeli independence, the Syrians had used the Golan Heights as a position from which to shoot at the kibbutzim in the upper Jordan Valley. Even certain members of Israel's left wing appreciated the vulnerability of the kibbutzim. They had been exposed to continuous harassment by Syrian snipers who shot at them from an extensive system of bunkers. The snipers gave kibbutz gravediggers more work than they ever wanted. The 1967 victory over Syria allowed Israel's farmers finally to plow their fields without fear of getting their heads shot off.

Syrians had never densely populated the Golan Heights. In addition to a few Druze villages, there was only one midsize town, Kuneitra, which was destroyed during the Six-Day War. Druze are not Moslems. They believe that Jethro, father-in-law of Moses, established their secret religion. Druze live in Israel, Lebanon, and Syria, and they have always been loyal to the country in which they live. (Later, when Israel invaded Lebanon in 1982, Druze patriotism resulted in some curious situations: Israeli Druze soldiers found themselves pitted against their Lebanese brethren.)

In the fighting for the Golan, few people were displaced by the Six-Day War. That fact and the strategic advantages of having the region under Israeli control made annexation palatable to most Israelis. The government of Menachem Begin formally annexed the Golan in 1983.

The West Bank and Gaza present a very different story, however, and how they should be handled remains a central concern of Israeli politics. Many of the Arabs who fled Israel's borders in 1948 ran to Gaza, a 30-mile long, 5-to-10-mile-wide strip of land that follows the Mediterranean coast to Egypt's border. In 1956 Gaza had been conquered by Israel. Israel's action was a response to the fedayeen terrorists who regularly mounted murderous raids from Gaza, as well as to Nasser's having closed the straits of Tiran, isolating Eilat, Israel's southern port on the northern shore of the Red Sea and her gate to the Indian Ocean and Asia.

Threatening to impose sanctions and hinting at the possibility of military intervention, the United States, under the leadership of President Dwight David Eisenhower, forced Israel to retreat from Gaza. U.S. assurances that it would never again allow Egypt to blockade the Straits of Tiran were hollow, and in May 1967, less than 11 years later, Nasser had once again closed the waterway. Within a few weeks, Israel recaptured Gaza in the Six-Day War.

Gaza has long been a hotbed of Egyptian radical activity, so most Israelis would be more than happy to see Gaza ruled by any country other than Israel. The Moslem Brotherhood, Egypt's most radical political group, had spread its fundamentalist ideology throughout Gaza even before the 1967 Israeli occupation. Movements, including Islamic Jihad and Hamas, formed during the 1970s, have the covert support of Iran. Their political and religious philosophies are completely aligned with those of Osama Bin Laden and his followers, who as long ago as February 1993, struck out against the West, driving a truck packed full of explosives into the World Trade Center garage. Investigators found Bin Laden's well-documented plans to wreak further havoc in New York City. But it's clear that his followers' eventual success on September 11, 2001,was far greater than even his wildest dreams.

The West Bank poses other problems. Although Gaza is certainly a part of biblical Israel, its historical importance and its impact on Judaism is dwarfed by Jews' collective religious memory of the West Bank names. For example, it was at Beth-el, the Bible tells us, that Jacob saw the angels climbing the ladder to heaven; Bethlehem was the birthplace of King David; Shiloh was the cultic sanctuary of the prophet Samuel; and Hebron is the site of the Tomb of the Patriarchs.

From a more mundane and practical point of view, it's important to note that the hills of the West Bank are dangerously close to the centers of Israeli population. Hostile control of these hills would have devastating effects on Israel's capacity to sustain any kind of normal existence for its residents.

Israel's leftist political parties, whose stance Nivi valiantly represented in our arguments, support the idea of a Palestinian state in the West Bank and Gaza. The parties on the right, however, insist that for reasons of security as well as historical continuity, these areas must remain under Israel's control. That, of course, is my position.

Unlike most of the other residents of Shavei Shomron, however, I never was a captive of the more fundamentalist Jewish philosophy represented by Gush Emunim. I was alone in my refusal to support groups that formed to prevent Israel's retreat from Sinai in 1982. Sinai, including the area around Yamit, eventually was returned to Egypt but not before massive rioting carried out not by the inhabitants of the area, who were financially compensated by the Begin government, but by members of Gush Emunim. They feared that returning the Sinai to Egypt and abandoning the settlements there would inevitably lead to the evacuation of their own West Bank and Gaza towns. Subsequent negotiations with Yasser Arafat prove that their apprehensions were well founded.

My concerns were much more pragmatic. Shavei Shomron is situated only 20 miles from the Mediterranean coast. I could easily see the coastal town of Natanya from the hills near my house. Having lived in Natanya for ten years prior to my move to Samaria, I could identify individual houses in the distance. On the basis of my military training as an artillery observer, I was keenly aware of the extreme strategic importance of these hills. The so-called experts from the left-wing political parties who claim that altitude has no strategic military consequence will never convince me that I am wrong.

In fact, I was more pessimistic than either my messiah-motivated neighbors or left-wing idealists like Nivi. I knew that the Arabs are driven to clear the Arab-Moslem world of infidel rule. I had studied Arab and Moslem history, but it had been my experiences with my Arab neighbors that taught me about the critical role Islam plays in their struggle against Israel.

Before the intifada started, foreign students who were working and studying Hebrew at various kibbutzim used to visit our field school on Saturdays. Because our strict observance of the Sabbath precludes driving them on tours of the area, we would spend the day engaged in discussion and study. One day, following my brief talk about the history of our region, one of the visitors, a recent graduate of U.C.L.A., asked me, "What do your Arab neighbors think of all this?"

"Why don't you ask them yourself?" I responded.

I pointed to the houses on the hill opposite our town, singling out the house of Adnan, the mukhtar, or "mayor" of Nakura, the neighboring Arab town. Speaking passable English, Adnan told the inquisitive student, "Zvi and I are very comfortable together. We frequently visit at one another's homes, but it is impossible for Jews to rule in a Moslem area. This goes against the Koran, and God will not allow it."

It is worth noting that Adnan was far from devout. He regularly drank beer even though Islamic law forbids imbibing. He did not fast during the month of Ramadan, and privately he scoffed at the growing number of Arab women who wore the traditional head coverings and long robes instead of Western-style clothing. Nevertheless, it is a basic tenet of Islam that Moslems must rule over infidels, and that principle was deeply woven into his psychological makeup.

Despite Nivi's left-wing political alignment, he and I shared a great affinity for the West Bank and its incredibly rich associations with ancient Jewish history. Shulamit Aloni, one of Israel's leading left-wing politicians, insists on referring to the Tomb of Joseph, a nearby site that is holy to both Jews and Moslems, as the "grave of a random sheikh." Admittedly, she made remarks like that one in response to Gush Emunim's initiatives to enhance the Jewish presence in the vicinity of the tomb. Members of Gush Emunim did manage to establish a yeshiva (Jewish seminary) there, and they were continually harassing the government and military authorities to allow them to establish an even greater foothold. Recently, that site was vacated after former Prime Minister Ehud Barak's decision not to attack the Moslem hordes who had seized control of the tomb allowed an Israeli soldier to bleed to death.

Politicians like Aloni can always find experts to support their opinions. Immediately after Aloni made her remarks about the "grave of a random sheikh," Meir Ben Dov, an archaeologist, penned a widely read newspaper article in support of the view that the gravesite is historically irrelevant. Most Israeli archaeologists, however, have the good sense not to mix science and politics, at least not in print.

Certainly nobody can confirm that Joseph of the Bible is buried in the location known as the Tomb of Joseph. And I don't really care whether Joseph is buried there or even whether he existed as a living, breathing person or was a figment of a biblical author's imagination. But I often wonder whether these Israeli left-wingers express the same kind of disdain for the antiquities they visit in Rome or Athens. Do they scoff so dismissively about the Greek and Roman ruins? I find it painful that the Israeli leftists reserve all their contempt for the traditions of their own ancestors.

Jews with any integrity, especially Jews living in the land of Israel, should understand that Zionism has its roots in the Bible. If the Jews had not cherished the Bible, Jewish identity would have ended up in the same historical graveyard as the Babylonians, Hittites, Sumerians, and other nations of antiquity. The Jews have survived only because they cherished this book for more than 2,000 years.

On this, Nivi and I agreed. And although for him the thought of returning this area to Arab rule was distinctly unpalatable, he maintained that there could be no peace until the Arabs had this land. I had one response to that: there can be no peace because of the Moslem inability to allow Jews to control any land Moslems consider to be theirs.

Our arguments weren't always so serious. Nivi enjoyed joking about some of the extremely religious residents of Shavei Shomron, and I delighted in reminding him of the picture of Stalin, hero of Hashomer Hatzair, that for many years had decorated the dining room of his kibbutz. But over the years of our friendship, our differences of opinion were dwarfed by our overriding common goal: doing everything possible to help Adam pursue his projects.

By the time I met Adam, he had already scanned about half of the area within the survey's borders. He had made his decision to begin the survey in the Dothan Valley on the basis of convenience. Located in the area of Samaria that is closest to his home, the Dothan Valley is but a 15-minute drive from his kibbutz.

Khirbet Hammam, in the Dothan Valley, was one of Adam's earliest discoveries. The pottery from that site indicated that it had been active for about 1,000 years, from the time of King Solomon, in roughly 975 BCE, through the wars against the Romans, 66 CE to 70 CE. The most impressive remains were from the Roman period. The Romans had surrounded the city, constructing a siege system identical to but older than the system at Massada. Because we conducted only two seasons of excavations, we don't really know what happened to the town's Jews. We found no signs that the city had been destroyed by the Romans. Instead, it appears to have been abandoned peacefully.

Adam had identified the site as Narbata, which is mentioned only once in the history of Israel. Josephus Flavius, a Jewish general turned Roman historian, refers to Narbata in his *History of the Jewish War*, which describes the Jews' first-century revolt against Rome. He reported that the sparks for the revolt were ignited in 66 CE in nearby Caesarea. The Jews, who had been forced to flee from persecution by the mainly Greek community, fled to Narbata. About Narbata's fate, however, Josephus tells us nothing.

The remains of the intricate siege system at the site give a clear indication of how determined the Romans were to capture the city. Adam's assumption is that the city was populated by Jewish Zealots, whose nearly successful revolt is described by Edward Gibbon in his *History of the Decline and Fall of the Roman Empire*.

But Adam's excavations took him much deeper into the history of that site. He identified the earliest phase of the site as Arruboth, one of three cities—Arruboth, Hepher, and Socho—that existed in the third district of Solomon (I Kings 4:10). In that era, the kingdom had been divided into 12 districts that had been defined for purposes of taxation: every district was responsible for supporting the monarchy for one month of each year. The Hebrew name Arruboth contains the same three consonants as Narbata. Apparently, over the years, the name evolved from the Hebrew to an Aramaic version. Aramaic was the vernacular in the land of Israel during much of the Second Temple Period.

Prior to the day in 1977 that Adam presented his findings to the Israeli Exploration Society, the body that represents Israel's archaeologists, Narbata had been identified as having been located at a small hill near Ma'anit, a kibbutz only two miles from Adam's house. Socho, had been identified as the modern Arab town of Shweika, which is a few miles south of Ma'anit, and Hepher had been located in the same vicinity.

Those identifications had been made back in the 1920s by Benjamin Mazar, a pioneer of Israeli archaeology. As a result of his work, the entire area is now known as the Hepher Valley. Mazar, one of the editors of the *Biblical Encyclopedia,* had been given the honor of leading the excavation of the area adjoining the Western Wall in Jerusalem after the Six-Day War. And for ten years, he had served as president of the Hebrew University in Jerusalem.

Although it had been he who had made the erroneous identification of Narbata and Hepher, he found Adam's presentation convincing. He was the first to rise and address the congress. "This young man is right," he announced, "and I have been wrong for 50 years."

That day marked the beginning of a strong bond of friendship: Adam gratefully accepted Mazar's offer of advice and counsel on the survey, and as the project progressed, Mazar praised Adam's work both privately and publicly.

The bond that connected Mazar and Adam would eventually extend to and include me.

*   *   *

According to rabbinic tradition, a principle of biblical interpretation is that the stories of the Pentateuch are not written in chronological order. Like the Bible, which is not bound by chronology, I have elected to release myself from its cords. My personal Exodus preceded the Genesis of this story—at least chronologically.

Exodus

You have seen what I did to Egypt; I carried you on
eagles' wings and brought you to Me. (Exodus 19:4)

For centuries, the biblical Exodus from Egypt has been one of the most universally appealing of all biblical narratives. And Moses' plea to Pharoah—Let my people go—has been a source of inspiration to struggling peoples throughout the world.

Several centuries ago, American colonists so intensely identified with the ancient Hebrews' yearning for liberty that they named their New World cities after such biblical towns as Bethlehem, Hebron, Jerusalem, Beth-el, Shiloh, and Zion. They quite emphatically viewed their settlement in North America as a new Israel.

The last years of the 19th and the early years of the 20th centuries bore witness to an exodus of Jews from Europe—an exodus of enormous dimensions. Seeking religious, political, social, and economic freedom, tens of thousands emigrated from czarist Russia. Many of them immigrated to the United States, where they got their first glimpses of the American Dream in the sweatshops of New York City. A small fraction of those who left Europe headed for the biblical Promised Land, to Palestine, then under control of the Ottoman Empire.

When near the end of World War I, the British gained control of Palestine, the early Zionists expected the tide of Jewish immigration to turn. They had good reason to be optimistic. On November 2, 1917, Lord Balfour had issued a decree advocating a Jewish homeland in Palestine. The so-called Balfour Declaration was by far the most significant support for such a venture since 520 BCE, when Persia's Cyrus the Great allowed the Babylonian Jews to return to Jerusalem to build the Second Temple.

Following the Balfour Declaration, Chaim Weitzmann, the leader of the Zionist movement who later became the first president of the State of Israel, and King Abdullah, grandfather of recently deceased Jordanian King Hussein, engaged in friendly and hopeful negotiations. The two met at the Paris peace talks when nationalist groups from all over came to plead their cause before the victorious Allies of World War I.

For his kingdom, Abdullah paid a small price indeed. His family, the Hashemites, came from Saudi Arabia, where they were contenders for the throne. However, the Wahabi tribe, which continues to rule Saudi Arabia, proved a formidable opponent, and Abdullah was forced to turn to the British for compensation. Asserting that the Hashemite Bedouin tribe could trace its ancestry to the prophet Mohammed, Abdullah felt sure that his tribe should have its own kingdom. Why not?

The savior of the Hashemites had turned up in Arab lands during the latter stages of World War I. T.E. Lawrence, known to moviegoers as Lawrence of Arabia, was a captain in the British intelligence service. He had been assigned to Saudi Arabia, where his mission was to create Arab resistance against the ruling Ottoman Turks. His military successes were few: he was responsible for blowing up a few hundred yards of the famed Hijaz railroad that linked Mecca to Turkey. Rewarding his support for their political goals, the Arabs generously provided Lawrence with a succession of young boys of the Hashemite tribe.

In return for such sexual favors, Lawrence bombarded the British Foreign Office with dozens of grossly exaggerated reports that described extravagant tales of sacrifice and bravery on the part of the Hashemites. Apparently, he was much more effective as a promoter than as a soldier. In its infinite wisdom, the British Foreign Office, which to this day has never been a friend to Zionism or Israel, gave Hashemites 78 percent of the land that only a few years earlier the Balfour Declaration had designated as the Jewish homeland. Abdullah's kingdom of Transjordan covered all the land east of the Jordan and north of Saudi Arabia, and it bordered areas the British and French had carved out for Iraq and Syria.

In 1951 a disgruntled Palestinian assassinated Abdullah in Jerusalem. His mad son, Tal'al, could not possibly assume the throne, so Abdullah's grandson Hussein, then hardly more than a boy, had to take over.

In my opinion, the most admirable accomplishment of Hussein's reign was his survival as Jordan's king for more than 40 years. He was the target of at least 16 attempts on his life. His tribe of Bedouin Hashemites comprise a scant 25 percent of Jordan's population, and most of the rest consider themselves Palestinians. Some of them have resided in Jordan for many generations. Many others are refugees who fled from Israel in 1948 and from the West Bank in 1967.

Jordan's social tensions are reminiscent of the conflict-plagued relationship between farmers and cowboys on the plains of 19th-century North America. Hussein's camel-riding Bedoins are analogous to cowboys, and the Palestinians to the farmers. Hussein managed to maintain his control over Jordan by allowing only members of his Hashemite family to fill sensitive military and governmental positions. Unlike the cowboys and farmers in sanitized Rogers and Hammerstein shows, the Bedouins and the Palestinians can't be friends. Whenever tensions came to a boil, Hussein shed his Western veneer, cruelly and vindictively eradicating resistance.

The notorious fury of Bedouin vengeance is well documented. Woe to the young Bedouin girl who engages in sexual activity. Even Bedouins who have been living in Westernized Israel for more than 40 years cannot refrain from acting on their "obligation" to protect their "family honor." They don't give a second thought to slitting the throat of a sister or cousin who has strayed—even though they know that for committing murder, they will spend an eternity in jail.

Hussein was responsible for the deaths of more than 20,000 Palestinians in September 1970, when, using Jordan as a launch pad for terrorist activities against Israel, the Palestine Liberation Organization threatened his authority. Jordan is the closest neighbor to the land where thousands of European Jews sought refuge after World War II.

Even after the Nazi's grabbed power in post-World War I Germany, Europe's Jews were, for the most part, apathetic about Zionism. Much of Europe's Jewish population was religiously observant, and they supported Agudat Israel, a political movement that was fiercely opposed to Zionists, whom they saw as atheist heretics. Members of my own family relate tales of their Agudat Israel rabbis who hounded them for even thinking about Zionism as a political option.

In present-day Israel, Agudat Israel's participation in political life is confined to its inevitable alignment with the coalition government—regardless of which party heads it. Detractors of Agudat Israel object to its ability to amass government funding that far exceeds its legitimate portion as a tiny fraction of the country's population.

One religious movement that started early in the 20th century, Mizrahi, was the forerunner of the current National Religious Party. It was the only religious movement to lend active support for Zionism.

The sad result of such internecine conflict was that instead of making their exodus and heading for the Promised Land, most of Europe's Jews ended up in Auschwitz and other Nazi terminals. And after the war, the majority of Holocaust survivors did their best to get to the United States. Indeed, only one of the surviving members of my family, which originated in Czechoslovakia, went to Israel. The rest, including me, then a 13-month-old baby, immigrated to the United States. After the horrors of World War II, my parents were happy to rear their children through blessedly uneventful lives.

On Sunday, May 28, 1967, at the age of 20, my life changed forever.

Until that day, I had virtually no knowledge about Zionism. My parents had sent me to Jewish day schools that pretty much ignored the existence of the Zionist movement. That Sunday I was just starting to enjoy my summer vacation from Brooklyn College of the City University of New York, where I had been studying political science. The cloudless blue sky and low humidity made for a perfect day. So I readily agreed when a girlfriend phoned and asked me to accompany her to a demonstration in support of Israel.

At that time, I knew little about the reasons for the demonstration. As we made our way into Manhattan, my friend gave me a short course in Middle East current events. She told me that Egypt's Gamal Abdel Nasser had closed the Straits of Tiran, repeating a belligerent move he had made in 1956. Since the closing of the waterway two weeks earlier, the entire military establishment of Israel had been mobilized. Israel's government had grown cynical about assurances from successive U.S. presidents that the United States would intervene should Egypt make such a move.

Nasser had started moving troops over the Suez Canal, across the Sinai desert, up to the Israeli border. The U.N. troops that had been stationed in Sinai since the

1956 war proved to be no obstacle. Nasser had only to rattle his armor, and Secretary General U Thant moved to vacate the premises. The U.N. "peacekeeping" force was as useful as the U.S. promises that had "guaranteed" Israeli passage through international waters.

Israel was forced to mobilize her reserve troops. Men up to the age of 55—a healthy chunk of Israel's workforce—are subject to reserve duty in the armed forces. A long-term mobilization of such magnitude would, therefore, prove an economic catastrophe. During that two-week period, the country's economy had ground virtually to a standstill, and there was no sign of relief in the future. War was in the air, and Israel's high-school students had been set to filling sandbags and digging thousands of graves to accommodate the expected casualties.

It was at that critical stage that for the first time, American Jewry awoke from its know-nothing slumber. Twenty-five years earlier, U.S. Jews had done little to stop Hitler's massacre of Europe's Jews. By 1967, more than two decades after the end of World War II, there should have been no doubt: Jews needed a sovereign homeland. Nevertheless, the extremes of Judaism—the ultrareligious on the right and the Reform on the left—wanted nothing to do with Israel. Pleased to back a winner, the Reform movement changed its position in 1967. For their part, the ultrareligious remain consistently opposed to the Jewish state.

Between those two extremes, most U.S. Jews were indifferent. Fewer than 3,000 U.S. Jews—equivalent to the population of a few apartment buildings in Brooklyn or Queens, New York—had immigrated to Israel during the 19 years between 1948 and 1967. In the headily optimistic years immediately following the Six-Day War, some 50,000 U.S. Jews would emigrate, but 80 percent of them would return to the United States within three years of their arrival in Israel.

Riding into Manhattan on my motorcycle, my friend and I found our way to the demonstration in Central Park. I parked my bike against a tree on Fifth Avenue and looked around. The meager assembly—a few thousand people, mostly children—milled around waving little blue-and-white Israeli flags as one after the other, a succession of speakers took the podium.

At first, I hardly took note of what any of them said, and I really had no idea who the speakers were. For me, it was just a pleasure to be out on such a beautiful summer's day. It wouldn't be long before New Yorkers would be suffocating in sweltering humidity. Little by little, however, the speakers were demanding and getting even my attention. I was amazed. Despite the wide range of organizations they represented, every speaker agreed with the others. Every speaker was appealing to U.S. President Lyndon Johnson to aid our beleaguered brethren in the Middle East.

But I also realized that not a single one of the speakers suggested that those of us who were standing and listening should support Israel with anything more than our money.

As I watched them drive up to the dais in their expensive cars, I started to grow angry. I imagined them returning to their penthouses and their suburban homes, complacently confident that they had fulfilled their responsibilities as Jewish "leaders."

The longer I stood there watching, the angrier I became. As a teenager, I had been driven to learn as much as I could about the Holocaust. My parents and relatives who had lived through the war in Europe refused to talk about their experiences, so I had combed the shelves of the public library, reading anything that might explain the enormity of the Nazis' crime against our people. As I stood in Central Park that beautiful Sunday afternoon, I couldn't help thinking that like the Jews of 20th century Europe, Israel was confronting a life-or-death crisis. Would the world once again stand by and watch as more of our brothers and sisters met their end?

In the years that have passed since that demonstration, I have seen both American liberals and the Israeli left turn their backs on Israel. They are way too quick to criticize what they believe is an undue influence of the Holocaust on Israeli political thought. Israel's quest for defensible borders has been termed "paranoia," an unhealthy state of mind that dwells excessively on the memory of Nazi persecution. The same sort of criticism views Israel's tough negotiating position as intransigence that is traceable to an aberrant siege mentality.

How else can Israel react to the hostile world that surrounds her? In 1990, when Iraq attacked Kuwait, the wealth of those members of the Kuwaiti elite who hadn't managed to escape became the targets of greedy Iraqis. Despite the enormous physical damage Kuwait suffered as a result of Iraq's invasion, the Kuwaitis themselves were never threatened with annihilation.

The fate of Israel, however, should it lose a war to the Arabs, is too terrible to imagine. I have seen with my own eyes the mutilated bodies of Israeli soldiers who were killed by Syrians in October 1973. The Syrian soldiers had ripped off the Israelis' genitals and stuffed them in the mouths of their corpses. Arab atrocities against Israelis, especially civilian women and children, have become so commonplace over the years that outside of Israel, they rarely merit headlines.

With the single exception of the United States, which under President Richard Nixon, staged an airlift during the Yom Kippur War in 1973, no Western nation has come to Israel's aid in times of crisis. Even that lonely example taught us unforgettable lessons.

Barely one generation after Hitler's nearly successful attempt to exterminate the Jewish populations of Europe, the United States was stymied in its attempt to deliver supplies to Israel. One after another, the nations of Europe denied permission that would allow U.S. Hercules and Galaxy transport planes to make an intermediate fueling stop. Finally, responding to enormous pressure, Portugal relented.

What motivated Nixon's willingness to help Israel is anybody's guess. Audiotapes of Oval Office conversations during Nixon's administration make it abundantly clear that he and his advisors—especially Billy Graham—had little use for Jews. In fact, Henry Kissinger, the token Jew in Nixon's Cabinet, did more damage than good to Israel during his tenure as secretary of state. Although in more recent years, Kissinger has assumed a friendlier posture toward Israel, his paltry support comes at least 30 years too late.

If Texas oilmen George Bush and James Baker had been in office in 1973, it's unlikely the United States would have troubled itself to come to Israel's aid. When a thousand Jewish-American leaders demonstrated in Washington, D.C., asking Congress to grant loan guarantees to Israel, Bush all but accused them of treason. That he would rebuke Irish-American citizens for their massive support for the terrorist Irish Republican Army is beyond imagination. Even German-Americans who supported the pro-Nazi Bund in the 1930s never encountered such intense presidential disapproval.

I am reporting well-documented history. These are the facts. Israel's concerns about her vulnerability to Arab attack are far from paranoid.

Back then, in 1967, as I stood in Central Park on that Sunday afternoon, my attention, which kept wandering from the long-winded, fund-raising platitudes of the speakers, was drawn to posters that had been fastened to nearby trees. The flyers were asking for volunteers who would fly to Israel to fill the workforce gaps that had been created when the reservists were put on active military duty.

Much to my own surprise, I knew in a moment that I had no choice: I had to go. I knew precious little about Zionism. Up to that day, my only association with modern-day Israel was a dim recollection that I had an aunt who lived with her family in Jerusalem. But that Sunday I knew that Israel was in crisis, and the nonchalance of the other Jews at the demonstration fueled the fires of my latent love for the Jewish homeland.

I was astonished that the speakers had so much faith in Lyndon Johnson. What could have made them think that he would intervene and help Israel? In my mind, it seemed a forgone conclusion that no Texan would do anything that might threaten U.S. relations with the oil-producing Arab world. I am sorry to say that so far, my assessments have not proved wrong.

Two days after that demonstration, I found myself making my way to the Park Avenue offices of the Jewish Agency. The Jewish Agency was the de facto predecessor of the State of Israel. And since the creation of the state in 1948, the bailiwick of the Jewish Agency has included overseeing immigration to Israel. As long ago as the days of the Talmud, Jewish tradition has viewed moving to Israel as a step up, and immigration to Israel is called aliya—the Hebrew word that means "going up." The Department of Aliya was handling the volunteers who were responding to the posters that had attracted my attention.

Quite by chance, I discovered that I had a connection with the U.S. director of this department. His home in Jerusalem was in the apartment building where my aunt was living. Initially, he attempted to dissuade me from going. He was quite certain that war was imminent. I was determined, however, and responding to my persistence, he helped me make the necessary arrangements. I purchased a ticket for an El Al flight that was scheduled to leave John F. Kennedy Airport the following Sunday, June 4.

As a traveler, I was completely naïve. This was to be my first airplane trip and my first venture beyond U.S. borders. Exactly one week after the Central Park demonstration, I was on my way to Israel, one of about 100 passengers—none of whom was older than 25.

I later learned that one week earlier, another El Al flight had ferried a similar number of young volunteers to Israel. I was both proud and disappointed that I was one of fewer than 200 U.S. Jews who, when the future of the State of Israel was in the balance, were willing to do more than make tax-deductible contributions. As a matter of fact, most donations didn't materialize until after Israel's victory, which inspired enormous pride in the Jews of the Diaspora. People like to back a winner.

Perhaps I shouldn't be so bitter. I can understand that parents with young children and elderly people might be in no position to volunteer more than a check. Still, in 1967 the community of U.S. Jews numbered six million. And about 20 percent of that population comprised young people between the ages of 18 and 30. We 200 volunteers were but a molecule—not a drop—in the bucket. Since then, I have considered the phrase Jewish-American Zionist to be an oxymoron.

Aboard the plane, most of the volunteers were so exhausted by the emotional turmoil of the previous week—for many of us, it was our first time away from home—that we were asleep within moments of takeoff. When we were awake, we subjected the El Al flight crew to a continuous barrage of questions. What, we asked them, was the true situation in Israel? Their pessimism, obviously grounded in bleak reality, silenced our eager enthusiasm, and we landed in Paris rather more somber than we had been when we left New York.

When we arrived in Paris on Monday, June 5, at 9:00 a.m., the Six-Day War was exactly five hours old. It was with that news that El Al's ground crew greeted our flight. Our immediate reaction was to race to the nearest newsstand. It didn't take us long to figure out that in our entire group only two of the girls knew enough French to help us interpret the news as reported in *Le Figaro* and *Paris Match*.

The heavy black headlines reported the news from Arab and Egyptian news agencies, which at the time, were the only sources of information. The Arabs, shouted the headlines, were in the process of destroying Haifa and Tel Aviv, and it was only a matter of time before the Zionist infidels would be brought to their knees and decapitated. We were devastated. Of course, there was no way for us to know it at the time, but Israel had forbidden the release of any news during the critical first 48 hours of the war.

About half of our group simply turned to the nearby Pan Am ticket booth and had boarded a return flight to New York within hours. I decided that I would wait to see how things developed.

Waiting in an airport, gives one a peculiar perspective on world events. As we sat there, we noticed that the terminal was filling up with two distinctive groups of passengers. There were crowds of Arabs arriving from Egypt and Jordan, notable for their haphazard dress: even as a first-time tourist, I could tell that they had left home in haste. And their obviously expensive clothing and jewelry marked them as the wealthy elite. The pampered rich are always the first to flee any threat to their lifestyle.

The second group of "refugees" arrived on the few civilian planes that had departed Israel earlier that morning. These people—nearly all of them Hassidic, ultrareligious Jews—had left Israel because they wanted to avoid a war they didn't consider was theirs. These are Jews who since the 1920s and 1930s, have been fighting Zionism. Since 1948 they have taken advantage of the hospitality of the Jewish state, but they are Israelis only so long as being so doesn't interfere with their way of life or put them in harm's way. An infamous agreement they crafted with David Ben Gurion, Israel's first Prime Minister, exempts their children from military duty, so they really have no reason to concern themselves with the outcome of Israel's wars.

As we sat in the terminal looking out the huge windows and waiting for something—anything—to happen, we noticed our plane being towed to a far corner of the field. Not knowing what was going on, we assumed that we were just going to be sitting and waiting for a really, really long time. As it turned out, France, the only country in the world that would sell weaponry to Israel, was loading the plane with a variety of much-needed military equipment. For lack of space in the luggage compartment, even unoccupied seats in the passenger cabin were carrying equipment and supplies that would certainly never meet U.S. Federal Aviation Authority safety standards for carry-on baggage.

We passed an agonizing 12-hour wait, drinking coffee. The El Al flight attendants offered us sandwiches that had taken on the flavor of their plastic wrappings. We were nervous and overwhelmed by our ambiguous situation. Despite the tension that everyone was feeling, however, the El Al crew members were calm, and they worked hard to reassure us. They stayed with us throughout the endless hours, fielding a steady stream of questions, most of them repetitive and petty. Israelis have a well-earned worldwide reputation for being abrupt, tactless, and abrasive, but in times of crisis, they respond with self-possessed composure. During my subsequent sojourn in Israel, I would experience this phenomenon of Israeli behavior whenever Israel's existence was threatened.

All regularly scheduled flights to Israel had been cancelled with the outbreak of hostilities. Only El Al afforded even the slightest chance of getting to Israel, and its flight schedule had been disrupted. Being in Paris, among the busiest media centers in Europe, I expected that a crowd of journalists from around the world would be lining up at the El Al counter.

I was wrong. A single journalist, Arnaud de Borchgrave, then a senior editor at *Newsweek* in Europe, joined our group. He was amiable and willing to chat with us, but he had no more information than we did. De Borchgrave arrived at about 1:00 p.m., and about one hour later, four very well-dressed French-speaking men sat down among us. Of the four, it was obvious to all of us that the oldest of them, a man in his late forties, was the leader. The El Al crew, who knew him, greeted him enthusiastically, "Bonjour, Monsieur le Baron."

Our newest traveling companion turned out to be none other than the Baron Edmond de Rothschild, scion of a family whose efforts on behalf of the Zionist movement are the stuff of legend. In the latter part of the 19th century, the grandfather of Baron Edmond had purchased huge tracts of land in Palestine, helping to establish the first industries. The baron's businesses, including a famous winery at Rishon le-Zion, were among the first that would employ the new Jewish immigrants. The contributions of the Rothschild family reach far beyond mere philanthropy. Family members maintain active interest in the success of the many projects they have backed, including the financing of the building that houses Israel's Knesset, or parliament, and its Supreme Court.

The baron was on his way to Israel to see firsthand what was needed and how he could help. I have no idea whether he had information that was unavailable to us. Perhaps he knew that the Israeli military was trouncing the Arabs. To us, his mere presence was reassuring, and somehow his being there turned the tide of our emotions. We all had pretty much the same idea: if Monsieur le Baron was determined to go to Israel, we would follow his example.

At 9:00 p.m., precisely 12 hours after we'd landed at Orly, we boarded the plane and flew up into the night sky over Paris. Strange cartons and boxes had been loaded in the rear of the passenger compartment, and before he had moved the plane even one inch, the pilot had instructed us that that part of the plane was strictly off limits.

Everyone knew that flying time between France and Israel is five hours. I calculated that we would be landing at 3:00 a.m. Israel time.

Once again, I was wrong. We'd been airborne just over two hours, when I sensed that the plane was swinging around and making a gradual descent. Once again, the pilot addressed the passengers. We would be making an unscheduled landing in Athens. Apparently, not long after our takeoff from Paris, two Iraqi MIG jets had managed to penetrate Israeli air space. One had managed to release a bomb that fell on the main street of Natanya, a coastal city on the Mediterranean some 20 miles north of Tel Aviv, causing considerable damage. The Israeli authorities were understandably reluctant to let us land under those circumstances.

It was close to midnight when we landed in Athens. The landing area was well lit, and as we made our way down the plane's metal staircase, we grew increasingly apprehensive. In addition to a considerable number of military jeeps surrounding us, at least 40 well-armed Greek soldiers stood with their submachine guns pointed at us.

In 1967 with Arab – especially Palestinian – air terrorism still one year in the future, high levels of security were rare in the airports of the Western world. Nevertheless, the soldiers hustled us into two waiting buses, which hauled us off to the courtyard of a jail. Without the efforts and connections of the baron, I can't even guess how long we might have languished in that Greek jail. We were all extremely relieved when, after three hours, we were released to a hotel near the shore.

Wondering about the origins of our hosts' openly antagonistic attitude, we learned that one week earlier, a group of Greek colonels had seized power, deposing the democratically elected government. Given permission to roam at will until 6:00 o'clock the next evening, we were more than slightly aware of the oppressive military presence. Perhaps the hostility we sensed at our arrival had more to do with the coup than with us.

With a green light to tour, I was ready to visit the Acropolis. Just before I set out, the pilot reported that he had been in contact with people in Israel, and they had informed him that Israel's air force had destroyed the Egyptian air force on the ground during the first three hours of the war. Furthermore, he reported, Israeli tanks were sweeping through Sinai almost uninterrupted. We were stunned and amazed, but everyone was eager to believe the news. About half of the 50 passengers who had made it as far as Athens decided to end their part in our mutual adventure, and they informed the El Al crew of their plan to return to the United States.

It was only when our diminishing group reported to the airport later in the afternoon that we learned the reason for our detour in Athens. The pilot had since received further confirmation of Israel's victory. He explained that as an unarmed civilian flight, our plane would require a military-jet escort, which would be available only at night. During daylight hours, the Israeli jets were fully occupied bombing the enemy.

Boarding the plane that evening, I was beginning to feel like a veteran flyer: unlike the takeoffs from New York and Paris, the departure from Athens did not leave me with my stomach in my throat. When we were two hours into the flight, the pilot clicked on the public-address system and instructed us to pull the shades over all the windows. At the same time, every light on the plane was turned off so that we wouldn't attract the attention of a stray Arab fighter jet. Within five minutes, our plane was shuddering—intensely tremendous noise and vibration on both sides had me convinced that I had seen my last day. As my life flashed proverbially before my eyes, I prepared myself for the worst. My anxiety turned to exaltation when the pilot informed us that the thundering jets that had surrounded us were, in fact, Israeli Mirage fighter jets that had been sent to escort us into Israeli airspace. They accompanied us until we descended for the landing.

Later, I learned that not only was the interior of our plane in complete darkness, but also all of Israel—the airport and runway, included—was maintaining blackout conditions. Due to the skill of our pilot, the other passengers and I had no idea that he was landing the plane onto an invisible runway.

Only when we were gingerly trying to make our way down the metal stairway to the tarmac did we realize that the lights were out all over Israel. In the virtually empty airport, it took only moments for the Israeli border police to process our passports. And we were surprised and relieved that despite our off-schedule arrival, a representative of the Jewish Agency was there to welcome us to Israel. We moved quickly to identify and collect our luggage, and we boarded a bus that would take us to Herzliya, a coastal town north of Tel Aviv, where we would spend the night.

I remember thinking how fortunate it was that there was no traffic: we drove with no headlights. Peering out the window, I could see nothing along the way. There were no lights at all. I had no idea whether we were driving through cities or traversing a rural landscape.

Arriving at a long, two-story building, a home for elderly that had been vacated temporarily when the staff had been called up for military service, we identified our luggage with the aid of small flashlights. Sleep was a welcome refuge from the tensions that had been building over the past week and especially the last two days.

A creature of habit, the next morning I rose at dawn. I was eager for my first glimpse of the Land of Israel. I stepped out of the tiny room I was sharing with a still-sleeping medical student from New York University and followed the aroma of coffee that was drifting up the hall from the reception area. On a small table next to the coffee machine, sugar, milk, spoons, and plastic cups were neatly arranged. I quickly drank a cup of coffee, set down my cup, and opened the glass doors to the Holy Land. (Years later, I learned that the Land of Israel had been dubbed the Holy Land by Christians during the Byzantine Period.) Being somewhat familiar with Israel's geography, I knew that Herzliya is just north of Tel Aviv. And keeping the rising sun behind me, I headed toward the sea.

The beach was only 200 yards from the building. That morning, the clean, clear scent of the sea air was overpoweringly heady, and the sky was bluer than any I had ever before seen. Within the next few years, however, air pollution from Israel's unregulated industries would cloud the sky and taint the air. That morning, the rumble of distant fighter jets cut through the early stillness of daybreak, but I felt a remarkable serenity as I gazed over the sea, marveling that I was actually in Israel.

The night before, when we were directed to our rooms, we had been told that our day would start officially at 6:00 a.m., so after taking a look at my watch, I reluctantly retraced my steps.

The Jewish Agency staffers who were our guides impressed us all with their matter-of-fact manner. Despite the war that was raging only a few miles away, they maintained the same businesslike attitude we had admired in the El Al flight crew. I would learn that this comfortingly reassuring approach that we had had the good fortune to enjoy is atypical to say the least. El Al personnel are known for being brashly abrupt, and the Jewish Agency is widely considered one of the world's most stifling bureaucracies.

When several far-from-modern buses pulled up in front of the building, our names and destinations were called out one by one. We had been allowed to choose either a religious or a nonreligious kibbutz. The small handful of volunteers who like myself had specified a preference for a religious kibbutz, went either to Kibbutz Yavne or Kibbutz Hafetz Haim. On the basis of its name, which means "will to live," I opted to go to Hafetz Haim. The kibbutz had been named after an exalted 20th century European rabbi who was renowned for the high regard and respect with which he treated people. The phrase comes from Psalms 34:13-15: "Who is the man who wills to live and covets the days, so he may see the good? (He who) curbs his tongue from evil and his lips from deceit. Turn away from evil and do good; seek and pursue peace."

I spent the next three months with people who, as a group and individually, strived to live their lives in accordance with the Psalms. I do not mean to say that the kibbutzniks of Hafetz Haim are perfect in every way. Still, I believe that their lives and their behavior bear the unmistakable imprint of sincere modesty.

Five of us had boarded a rickety old bus that made me think that the trip south to Kibbutz Hafetz Haim might be its last. I'm certain that only divine intervention kept it from falling to pieces along the road. As we made our way, I tried to imagine what kind of life I would find there, but I was completely unprepared for Malka Zeliger, the tiny, middle-aged woman who greeted us. The diminutive mother of five was in charge of all volunteers who made their way to the kibbutz. Although she was small, she was a force that could not be denied. Within minutes of our arrival, she had herded all of us to the kibbutz dining room, and we were eating food that none of us was hungry enough to want.

It took no less than half an hour to convince her we hadn't come to eat: we were ready to be useful. We stowed our luggage in the ramshackle rooms that were assigned to us, and Malka took us to meet Adler. Like most of the strictly observant men of his generation, Adler was bearded. For the most part, the younger kibbutzniks were beardless, but almost all of them sported drooping mustaches.

Adler was in charge of labor assignments. Within the hour, I found myself wearing the kibbutzniks' standard uniform: navy-blue work shirt and trousers. Except for the pallor that marked me as a recent arrival, I was pleased to note that I looked like everyone else on the kibbutz. Adler motioned that I should follow him, and at the end of a 15-minute walk, we arrived at an apple orchard, and I was handed over to Shalom Goldman, who was a philosophy professor from New York University. Although he had arrived only one week earlier, he was already a veteran apple picker, and he had acquired a deep tan that made him indistinguishable from the natives.

He showed me the right way to pick the apples, and I began to work on the tree next to his. We barely spoke. He took his work very seriously, and so did I.

That was Wednesday, June 7, 1967. A continuous stream of fighter planes from the neighboring air-force base of Tel Nof cracked the normal silence of the orchard. They were engaged in nonstop bombardment of Egyptian and Jordanian forces.

The sun shone fiercely, and as we picked the apples, we'd take brief breaks to drink cool, refreshing water from our canteens. I'd been there for about two hours when at 11:50 a.m., my attention was grabbed by sounds of one of Israel's French-made Mirage jets buzzing through the air like an excited bumblebee. Back and forth, up and down. The flapping of the wings, said Shalom, who in my eyes was already an expert, meant either that the pilot had downed an enemy plane or that he had received momentously good news.

Shalom reached for his knapsack, which was lying at the foot of his tree, and he extracted a tiny transistor radio. The two of us waited impatiently for the series of beeps that marks the beginning of hourly news broadcasts. We were not disappointed.

The announcer, whose voice I soon learned to identify as belonging to Reuma Eldar, reported that Israeli paratroopers had captured the Old City of Jerusalem, site of the only remnant of Israel's Second Temple, the famed Wailing, or Western, Wall.

Since 1948 Jordan had denied Jews access to the wall, and its capture in the Six-Day War can accurately be described as the most uplifting moment in the past two millennia of Jewish history. Jews from all parts of the world, regardless of their particular beliefs or backgrounds, rejoiced with Israel on that day. *Har habayit beyadeinu!* "The Temple Mount is in our hands!" exulted Motta Gur, then commander of the paratroop division that captured the Old City. Gur later became commander-in-chief of Israel's Army.

Within ten minutes of that radio announcement, small children came running breathlessly from the center of the kibbutz. "Stop working," they cried. "We're preparing to celebrate."

Life was happening so fast that I had to catch my breath. I could hardly believe where I was, and I was amazed to be in the midst of such activity. A party! I had been working for less than three hours, and they're throwing a party! I realized, of course, that at this religiously observant kibbutz, the idea of a party would not mean disco dancing.

Shalom and I emptied our plastic buckets of apples into a large container for pickup by the tractor that would make its rounds of the orchard later in the day. We returned to our rooms to shower and put on fresh blue uniforms. We would have blended in pretty well with the rest of the kibbutzniks, but being among the very few men between the ages of 18 and 55, we did feel odd. The seven male volunteers—six from the United States and one from France—were virtually the only males in that age category on the entire kibbutz.

The party turned out be more like a ceremony than a gala. Tables set up outside the synagogue were covered with white tablecloths, and a variety of fruit, cakes, and drinks were there for the taking. The entire kibbutz—from newborn babies to the elderly and infirm in wheelchairs—filled the wide lawn in front of the synagogue.

When a bearded man wearing black hat, black suit, and thick round glasses rose and started to speak, the crowd fell silent, and everyone listened with complete attention. Later, I learned that that day's speaker had been Rabbi Kalman Kahane, who at the time was a member of the Knesset for the Po'alei Aguda Party, the movement to which Kibbutz Hafetz Haim belonged. This ultrareligious party is fiercely Zionist, and unlike many other ultrareligious groups, its young people do not study in yeshivas in lieu of fulfilling the responsibilities of military service.

Most of the kibbutz men were in fighting units, and almost all of them were paratroopers. And despite the complete lack of contact between the men at war and their families back in the kibbutz, we were celebrating. No one could know whether there were any injured or dead among their members who were fighting on the three fronts of the war.

Personal considerations had been swept aside that day. Everyone celebrated the capture of the Old City of Jerusalem. Rabbi Kahane spoke for two hours, barely giving mention to the war. He spoke almost exclusively about the centrality of Jerusalem in Jewish history. King David, King Solomon, and Jeremiah the prophet were the heroes of whom he spoke.

I was gratified that I already knew enough Hebrew to follow Rabbi Kahane's speech. Like me, everyone was rapt. None of the hundreds of people gathered there uttered a word. Even the infants seemed aware of the awesome power of the day. None of them let out even a whimper while he spoke.

At the conclusion of his speech, everyone returned to work. That evening, I managed to phone my aunt in Jerusalem. I wanted to let her know where I was and to find out how she and her family were coping with the war. I promised that after the war, I'd visit at the first opportunity.

I was able to fulfill my promise that very Sunday. With the capture of the Golan Heights from Syria, the war was over on Saturday. Still, transportation for civilians was severely limited, and the trip to Jerusalem, which normally took an hour and a half, took more than four hours.

I was about ten minutes outside of Jerusalem when the police ordered my bus and all other cars, trucks, and buses traveling to Jerusalem to pull over to the right side of the narrow, bumpy road. Stopped at the top of a hill known as the Kastel (the site of one of the most famous battles of Israel's War of Independence), I could see the outlines of Jerusalem. Traffic had been stopped along the road, as far as the eye could see.

Within moments, we saw what was delaying the traffic. Dozens of tanks that had been captured from the Jordanian soldiers were being driven to a military depot near Tel Aviv. All the travelers—from the buses, cars, and trucks that had been waiting—stood alongside the road cheering, and we all wept with pride and joy.

When finally my bus pulled into the Central Bus Station, I climbed down and started to search for the number 15 bus that my aunt had told me would take me to her house. My confusion attracted the attention of an elderly couple who had two small grandchildren in tow. They addressed me in Yiddish, and when I told them what I was looking for and where I was headed, they said that I should follow them.

Only once we had all boarded the number 15 bus, did they admit to me that they had been headed in a completely different direction and that because they were worried that I might get lost, they had decided to accompany me to my destination. Coming from New York, a city that is notorious for its indifference to its own, much less to strangers, I was overwhelmed by their kindness and generosity of spirit.

They told me when to get off the bus and directed me toward my aunt's street. Walking up her street, I felt the reality of the war. Jordanian artillery shells had left huge craters in the road, and any window that hadn't been taped, was broken. Shards of glass were everywhere.

My cousin Zvika, two years my junior, was with a friend studying for the high school matriculation examinations. Throughout the week of war, the two friends had studied in a bomb-proof shelter. Now that the war was over, they were outside, and, as I walked up the street, Zvika recognized me from family photos. He ran to greet me and guided me to my aunt, who was at work, just across the road.

The big plate-glass windows of the relatively new building where my aunt taught cosmetology had been shattered by the bombs. Millions of tiny glass splinters covered the tile floors like a glittering carpet. We found Aunt Pnina wearing her white uniform and standing in the middle of this mess, broom in hand, attempting to rectify the situation. She wouldn't wait for the regular cleaning crew to return from the army.

The moment I appeared, she started asking questions about our large family in New York. I found that she couldn't pause—even for my answers! And as I look back on the more than 30 years that have passed since that day, I think that I am still waiting for my chance to speak. I wanted to ask her about how she and her family had fared during the fighting and about the kind of lives they lived in Jerusalem. It was she who had experienced a week in a war-torn city—not her U.S. brothers, sisters, and cousins about whom she had so many questions. My own questions had to wait until we had returned to her house. My uncle Shlomo's job had taken him to England, and the family had spent three years there, so it was easy to converse with them in English.

Like all the other Israelis I had met so far, my family members were all completely blasé about the war. Israelis, I was discovering, respond well to stress. My visit lasted a few hours, and then I made my way back to the kibbutz. The next few weeks were far less eventful than the days I had spent since May 28, but I was learning my way around the kibbutz, and I was thrilled to be there. Gradually, the men were returning from the army, and for the weeks and months to come everyone was hungry for their stories about their experiences of the war.

It didn't take me the full three months I was on the kibbutz to realize that I was at home in Israel. I decided that within my first month there. I was not so naïve as to believe that the Israelis would sustain forever the remarkably good spirits that were the result of the war. Furthermore, anybody could see that despite the stunning victory, Israel was still surrounded by aggressively hostile Arab countries. And their enmity was eternal.

Nevertheless, I knew as well as a person can ever know anything that Israel is the only place on earth where a Jew can experience a real sense of identification with his race and a true feeling of national unity, pride, and community.

I had crossed the Sea of Reeds, and I was finding my way in the Promised Land.

The remarkably selfless behavior that characterized the entire population during the Six-Day War faded in time, but one always catches shadows and glimpses of it hovering in the background. From time to time, I am overcome by feelings of pessimism about the weaknesses and failings of Israeli society. Invariably, however, I have to admit that in all phases of Israeli life, there is always an undercurrent of concern for the common good.

My Exodus was complete. Or so I thought.

Leviticus

*And God spoke to Moses saying, "Command Aaron
and his sons, and say that this is the law of the
burnt offering." (Leviticus 6:1-2.)*

The third book of the Pentateuch, Leviticus, is so named because much of it is devoted to discussion of the activities performed by the priests and Levites. Most of those activities were related to functions performed in the *mishkan,* the portable sanctuary, or tabernacle, which was constructed by the Israelites in the wilderness. The mishkan was the forerunner of the Temple of Israel.

People are surprised to learn that I have always found Leviticus to be the most fascinating book of the Bible. Rather than being bored by and uninterested in the extensive descriptions, prescriptions, and proscriptions associated with priestly activities, I am fascinated by the narrative's marvelous record of cultural development. Leviticus comprises the main part of a larger biblical work known in Hebrew as *Torat Kohanim,* or Laws of the Priests. Parts of Exodus and Numbers also deal with these topics, and most scholars ascribe those additional texts to the same biblical source.

What we found at Mount Ebal led me to examine a broad range of historical, geographical, physical, and literary source materials, many of them relating to the Laws of the Priests. My interdisciplinary approach may initially seem fragmented, but in the end, you will see that the various aspects of my research unite to form a solid and coherent picture.

In this chapter, I escort you along the path I followed. Some of that path will be very obvious and easy, but the complex twists and turns of other parts will demand your patience. First, I will introduce what was possibly the greatest moment of my life, the moment we began to understand the Ebal site. Then I will present the questions that I needed to answer in order to reach my conclusions. Some of the answers overlap and relate to more than one question. So take a deep breath, and let's begin the journey. I'm sure that by its end you'll agree that it was worth the trip.

*   *   *

My first meeting with Adam was the beginning of a long and fruitful friendship. From that day onward, we met frequently. To strengthen his legs, which were brutally injured by enemy bombs when he fought in the Yom Kippur War, Adam does an extraordinary amount of walking every day, and I liked to join him on his strolls along the hedge-lined lanes of his kibbutz. I never tired of listening to him describe the results of his survey. The chief focus of almost all our conversation was one particular site that Adam had discovered in the vicinity of the ancient city of Shechem, which is visible to this day in the remains of *Tel Balatah* on the eastern edge of the Arab city Nablus. That site was located on the eastern side and just below the top of Mount Ebal, the highest peak in northern Samaria.

The Mount Ebal site, Adam told me, consisted of a central pile of stones—remnants of ancient walls that rise out of the soil that surrounds the pile—and thousands of pottery shards that are strewn over the entire area. He was intrigued by the remarkable homogeneity of the shards: nearly all of them were from the earliest stage of the Iron Age, known as Iron I. There were also a few shards from the Late Bronze era, which preceded and overlapped Iron I.

The Iron Age in Israel started in the 13th century BCE, at the time of the Settlement Period, with evidence of the appearance of the Israelite tribes. The entire age lasted through the destruction of the First Jerusalem Temple, in 587 BCE. Archaeologists trace the first stage, Iron I, through the beginning of the monarchy of the House of David, around 1000 BCE.

Adam was very excited by the overwhelming number of shards: their presence indicated that the location had been the center of considerable activity. Yet the remnants of the ancient walls showed no signs of having been part of residential construction. Furthermore, the walls formed two concentric enclosures whose dimensions were not at all consistent with walls that were built as protection against intruders. What would have been the purpose of a site that was neither a residential town nor a defensive fortress? Quite possibly, Adam explained to me, it might prove to be the most fascinating of all archaeological discoveries: a cultic site.

The unearthing of almost any cultic site can drive an archaeologist wild with the passion to excavate. Imagine then, Adam's reaction: he had found what might be a cultic site in Israel. And not just anywhere in Israel, but in Mount Ebal, a place that is mentioned in the Bible. What if the site yielded artifacts that could be tied to that biblical text? Such a find would be the first direct connection between an archaeological artifact found in Israel and the text of the Five Books of Moses. And there were tantalizing hints that we might have the ingredients for making such a connection: In each of the two biblical mentions of Mount Ebal, there is reference to a ceremony—a cultic event—performed by Joshua. Furthermore, scholars agree that Joshua lived during the early stages of Iron I, the period to which we had dated all the Mount Ebal pottery shards!

As we traced the pathways around his kibbutz, Adam told me that he had come to that site for the first time on April 6, 1980, about a year and a half before the two of us met for the first time. He was extremely eager to get started on the excavation of the site, and his enthusiasm and curiosity were so contagious that I couldn't stop trying to come up with ways I could help him accomplish this task.

I reviewed the vast array of hurdles that he would have to overcome in order to proceed, and I admit that they seemed insurmountable. First of all, an excavation calls for considerable capital. Not only would Adam need to recruit staff, he'd eventually have to pay wages. He would, of course, need trained archaeologists, each of whom would be assigned responsibility for specific loci—the squares that were designated for excavation. A photographer would have to shoot all the loci at the end of each day, documenting special finds, as well as the entire site from various angles. A professional draftsman would have to draw detailed pictures of all the walls and a topographic design of the entire site. These are but a few of the fundamental and lightest expenses that are part and parcel of any excavation.

Really, a most critical aspect of such ventures is the feeding, housing, and providing of transportation for the volunteers every day of every week for the duration of the excavation. Only expeditions that achieve fame and glory can expect volunteers who are committed and eager to pay their own way. In addition to the day-to-day costs of running an excavation, every project incurs residual expenses and the need to spend money on a continuous stream of odds and ends.

As he described his burning desire to pursue this excavation, Adam admitted that the daunting realities of the logistics and expense were starting to douse the fire of his enthusiasm. For my part, I was pleased to have an opportunity to offer expertise of my own. I told him that my experience in hotel administration, in which I had earned an academic degree and at which I had worked for more than a decade, could serve him well. He accepted my offer to draw up a complete plan for one "season" that would account for all project needs and their costs.

A season generally lasts from two to six weeks, depending on the availability of time, money, and other resources. Planning for an excavation that would last four weeks, I estimated that Adam would need $15,000 to $20,000. That amount, though paltry compared to the vast sums laid out for certain archaeological ventures in Israel, was still far more than Adam could possibly afford. It had been 18 months since his discovery of the Ebal site, and assuming that his fundraising efforts would be futile, he had made virtually no effort to arrange for an excavation.

Lack of funding was only one of many substantial problems that stood in Adam's way. The Ebal site is, as I've mentioned, located near the biblical city of Shechem, which is 500 yards east of the center of Nablus, a very nationalistic Arab city. How could Adam, a member of a Shomer Hatzair kibbutz, initiate a dig in the heart of Arab territory on the West Bank? Some of his fellow kibbutzniks would certainly object to such a project. Furthermore, Islamic fundamentalism had bred terrorism that posed a distinct and significant threat to volunteers, who would need to commute to work by bus in the vicinity of Nablus. Finally, Adam had only recently earned his master's degree in archaeology. He was still years away from a doctorate, and a doctorate certainly has a positive influence on fundraising.

Despite these rather daunting odds, Adam and a group of volunteers, which included me, embarked on our first season of excavation in April 1982, just a few months after Adam and I first met. I had solved many financial and logistical problems by making my town's field school, Midreshet Shomron, the base of operations. All crew and volunteers slept there, and its kitchen supplied their food.

It takes time to acclimate and adjust to the vagaries of any site, and because our first season was only four weeks long, we did not have much to show for it. But two findings served to sustain our enthusiasm:

First, we found pieces of bone that encouraged us and sustained our belief that we were working at a cultic site. Of course, bones are likely finds at any domestic site as well. But all the bones we found, even at that very early stage, were the type that can be described as potentially cultic: they showed signs of having been burned on an open fire, and they were the bones of animals the Bible designates as appropriate for sacrifice.

Second, we determined that the large pile of stones located at the center of the site was covering something. As we removed the top layer of that pile, we saw a systematic arrangement of stones that indicated the presence of walls. Admittedly, a large pile of stones is far from rare on the mountainsides of Samaria. Before the local farmers can cultivate their fields, they have to dig up literally tons of stones and move them aside. As a result of centuries of farming, therefore, one sees stones heaped on almost every hillside field of Samaria. But the pile we were examining was distinctly different from those of the farmers: our pile of stones was surrounded by thousands of pottery shards.

*   *   *

With such persuasive indications that our site was indeed a cultic site, we devoted the next six months to the fundraising and logistical challenges prerequisite to another season. We had learned from our experiences—and our mistakes, and we were certain that the second and subsequent seasons would progress more smoothly than the first.

As it turns out, however, we made modest progress during the second season, the following October. Although our excavations revealed more of the structure that was under the pile of stones, we were nowhere near ready to smoke the celebratory cigar.

It was the third season of excavation, in October 1983, that despite a slow start, was to be most memorable. Even though we had uncovered many features of the central structure, by the second week of that season, we had yet to see any clear indication of its purpose. Our work had to progress extremely slowly because the walls of the structure had been built of ordinary fieldstones that were almost indistinguishable from the stones that had been covering the structure itself. Nobody lifted a stone from the central structure without Adam's overseeing and approving the move.

Almost every evening, Adam and I sat sipping coffee on the lawn in front of his room in the field school facilities. From there, he could supervise the volunteers as they washed the pottery found during the day.

Days at the dig started with a wakeup call at about 3:30 a.m., so that the bus and jeep could get everyone to the site by 5:00 a.m. We worked until 1:00 or 2:00 in the afternoon, and then we returned to the field school for lunch. Following the afternoon siesta, the workers reassembled at about 4:30 or 5:00 to wash the pottery they'd unearthed earlier in the day. To loosen the centuries of accumulated dirt from the pottery, the volunteers soaked the pieces in buckets of water and scrubbed each one with small, tough brushes. Until the shards had been cleaned, it was impossible to catalog them.

One evening as we sat chatting about this and that, Adam handed me a sketch he'd been working on. He had been doodling with a pencil, drawing designs on a sheet of paper. As he passed it to me, he told me that his picture was a diagram of the structure he expected our excavations would soon reveal. Not even interrupting the story I was telling him, I reached for the page, looked at his sketch, and then, gasping in surprise, leapt to my feet, shouting, "I'll be right back! Wait here!"

I raced to the extensive library in Shavei Shomron's synagogue and headed straight for the book I wanted. Returning to a bemused Adam, I opened the book and passed it to him. Now it was Adam's turn to be stunned. The illustration on the page I showed him was nearly identical to his drawing (see appendix, pages 184 and 185).

The book I had retrieved was a volume of the Mishnah, the oldest part of the Talmud. Most of the Mishnah's sources were texts that had been written in the three centuries immediately preceding its compilation around 200 CE. For much of that period and up until 70 CE, when the Romans destroyed it, the Second Temple stood in Jerusalem. Naturally, large portions of the Mishnah, including the volume that I had brought to show Adam, discuss Temple-related activities.

The volume contained the tractate Midot, or "measurements" of the Temple and its contents; and that particular edition included diagrams that had been drawn to the specifications mentioned in the text of the Mishnah. The two of us sat there gazing at the book, which I had opened to a diagram of the altar of the Second Temple. The structure that was slowly emerging from the earth at Mount Ebal was astonishingly similar to the book's diagram. Dumbfounded and in mute agreement, we realized that "our" structure was a burnt-offering altar—the first to be discovered in the land of Israel.

That our site had been a cultic site was, as I've mentioned earlier, in itself very exciting. That it appeared to contain the first burnt-offering altar found in Israel was quite remarkable. But the much, much more astonishing revelation was that the location of the altar, the date of the altar, and the characteristics of the altar all correspond to the description of Mount Ebal that is found in Deuteronomy, the fifth of the Five Books of Moses, as well as to the description in the subsequent biblical book of Joshua. Our having recognized the connection between the altar at Mount Ebal and those biblical texts called for a cigar. And what a cigar!

Immediately, Adam and I started to review what we had found, comparing it with the biblical texts.

In Deuteronomy, Moses commands the Israelites to perform a very unusual and highly detailed ceremony upon their entry into the land of Israel.

The ceremony was a three-part affair:

• An altar was to be built at Mount Ebal, and animal sacrifices were to be offered there. (Deuteronomy 27:5-7.)

• The word of the law was to be written on stones at the site. (Deuteronomy 27:8.)

• The 12 tribes of Israel were to split into two camps. Six tribes would stand on Mount Gerizim, and six would stand on Mount Ebal. (Deuteronomy 27:12-13.) And the priests and the Levites would recite a series of curses and blessings from the valley in between. The blessings would be for those who followed the word of the Lord, and the curses would be for the rest of us. (Deuteronomy 27:15-28:14.)

Joshua succeeded Moses as Israel's leader, and it was he who led the Israelites into the land of Israel and fulfilled Moses' command to perform the ceremony. One particular sentence in the book of Joshua grabbed our attention and fueled our enthusiasm: *Then Joshua built an altar to the Lord, God of Israel, in Mount Ebal.* (Joshua 8:30.)

The place was certainly right: Mount Ebal has been known by that name for at least 2,700 years. The Samaritans—a people first mentioned in the book of Kings as having arrived in Samaria following the Assyrians' destruction of the northern Kingdom of Israel between 723 BCE and 720 BCE—have preserved Mount Ebal's name. Their continuous existence in the same place is confirmed by their subsequent appearance in the New Testament, especially in the famous tale of the Good Samaritan.

Modern day Samaritans believe that they are descended not from transplanted Assyrians who converted to Judaism, but directly from the tribes of Joseph. Today in modern Israel, some 300 Samaritans live in Nablus, where the life of their tiny community is focused around their synagogue. There is a second community of Samaritans in Holon, just south of Tel Aviv. During the 19 years between the War of Independence and the Six-Day War, the West Bank was in Jordanian hands, so the two groups were incommunicado. After the war, Holon's Samaritans resumed their custom of celebrating their holidays, including Passover, atop Mount Gerizim. (It is Mount Gerizim to the south and Mount Ebal to the north that form the valley in which Nablus, on the site of ancient Shechem, is found.) The Samaritans have always regarded Mount Gerizim as their spiritual center, and during the Second Temple Period, they built a temple there that was similar to the Jerusalem Temple.

There is no question that the Samaritans have been present in the area for at least 2,700 years, and their presence has preserved the identity of many sites in the vicinity—including Mount Ebal. Consequently, there is also no question that Ebal is indeed the right place. Next, we considered whether what we had found could be dated to the right time.

Scholars mark the 13th century BCE as the beginning of the Settlement Period. The pottery we discovered at the Mount Ebal site is clearly identifiable as having originated in that period. And over the course of next several seasons, our excavations unearthed further proof: two scarabs and a seal.

A scarab is a beetle-shaped, semi-cylindrical oblong, flat on one side and rounded on the other, much like half an egg sliced lengthwise through its center. In the ancient world, scarabs were used as personal stamps. Most of them were no bigger than one inch long. We had found the tiny chalk stone seal, the size of a bottle cap, and the scarabs by sifting every bucket of earth through a strainer.

Taking extreme care to avoid making any false identifications, Adam sent the two scarabs and the seal to Baruch Brandel, a leading Egyptologist at the Hebrew University in Jerusalem. Brandel identified the three objects as dating to the reign of Ramses II. Ramses II is said to have ruled Egypt from 1290 through 1226 BCE, a period that coincides precisely with the Settlement Period. Historians including W.F. Albright, one of the pioneers of archaeological research in Israel, maintain that Ramses II was the Pharaoh to whom Moses declared, "Let my people go!" (Of course, there are also historians who insist that the Exodus never happened.)

One of the two scarabs, because it was decorated with a cartouche, made our find even more exciting (see appendix, page 183). Cartouches were the personal symbols of Pharaohs. The cartouche that appears on the scarab we had unearthed is among several known to have been used by Ramses II. Clearly, our find was momentous, and I equated it with the possibility that archaeologists 10,000 years from today might dig up a credit card that once belonged to Bill Clinton or George Bush.

Not only were we excavating in the right place, we were also in the right time period. Now we had to make sure that the central structure beneath the piles of stones really was an altar.

What is an altar? What should an altar look like? In academic circles, these questions, simple as they may appear, are very serious questions indeed. Physical evidence of ancient altars is scarce. Wars and religious reforms have destroyed all but a few altars in Israel and its neighboring countries. And of those few Israelite altars that have been discovered, none has been identified as an altar for burnt offerings. Rather, they have all been smaller, incense altars.

In ancient times, animal sacrifice was a commonplace expression of service to the deity. Noah built an altar and sacrificed animals when his floating zoo landed on Mount Ararat. Abraham, who very nearly sacrificed his son Isaac, made a habit of offering animals, as did the other patriarchs. But despite the many references to altars and obligatory burnt offerings, the Bible provides no specific blueprints that define the construction of an altar.

There are, however, guidelines. For the most part, we believe, altars were made of stone. For example, in Exodus 20:22, God commands the Israelites to build an altar of uncut stones. Iron, which might have been used to shape stone into manageable blocks, is also the tool of war, and therefore, according to the Bible, iron is unsuitable for building a structure that would be considered a symbol of peace between God and man. So we knew that the Bible specifically forbade the use of hewn stone.

Without a doubt, the central structure at the Mount Ebal excavation was made of uncut, natural fieldstones. So far, so good.

In Exodus 20:23, God's command continues, adding that there should be no steps for ascending to that altar. At our site, we had discovered a ramp that led from ground level to the top of our structure. No steps. Still good.

The base of the central structure is nine meters long and seven meters wide, and it rises to a height of three meters. Three meters is equal to ten biblical cubits, the height prescribed for every altar for which the Bible specifies dimensions. No matter its length or width, the height of every biblical altar was to be ten cubits. A critical point.

As we exposed the structure, we were able to see an inner wall of huge stones. An outer wall, built to half the height of the inner wall, surrounded it on three sides. The outer wall, roughly one meter wide, created a ledge wide enough for a man to walk on.

Did the outer wall serve some structural purpose? We asked architects, who told us that they could see no architectural necessity or logic for that wall. It did not support the inner wall, which supported itself very well. The fact that the wall was on only three sides of the structure—the side with the ramp and the two sides that adjoin the ramp—implied that it was meant to provide access to each of the four corners of the structure.

The biblical narrative describes the duties of the priests, focusing particular attention on the sprinkling of sacrificial blood at the corners of the altar. Although the Bible does not describe how the priests should reach the corners, it seems quite reasonable that they would walk along a ledge like the one we found at Mount Ebal. Furthermore, the stony ledge at Mount Ebal is a perfect match for the description of the ledge alongside the altar of the Second Temple, which was pictured in the book I had brought from the synagogue library.

Our excited voices filled the night air as we compared our findings with the Mishnaic text and the accompanying diagram. We were convinced that "our" structure at Ebal was indeed the structure that is described in Deuteronomy and Joshua.

The right time, the right place, and the right item. What we had dared only to dream was looking more and more like a real possibility.

Adam was cautious about spreading the news beyond the members of our crew. The first person he phoned was Professor Benjamin Mazar, who had served for a decade as president of the Hebrew University in Jerusalem and had chaired various departments at the University. He had also directed the excavations at the Western Wall in Jerusalem after the Six-Day War of 1967. Adam's news excited Mazar, who despite having been retired for several years, expressed eagerness to view our site. Adam suggested that we provide transportation for him, and I agreed to drive to Mazar's home in Jerusalem and bring him to the site the following morning.

I, however, wasn't finished for the night. I'd have to rise even earlier than normal for the roundtrip to Jerusalem, but I knew that I was far too wound up for sleep. That night, I embarked on what has stretched into a 15-year search for all information that might have a connection to our discovery. First, I turned to the traditional Jewish commentaries on the Bible, looking at texts that relate to the specific chapters that mention Ebal, as well as those that describe the Settlement Period and cultic activities connected with altars.

More than five hours passed without my realizing it. My extreme excitement precluded all but a most haphazard search for anything even remotely related to the subject. Racing through dozens of volumes, unable to focus or concentrate, I retained almost nothing from that night's "research."

The next morning, I was at Mazar's door at 7:00 a.m. Although for many people that seems a barbarously early hour, it's pretty late in the day for archaeologists. In any case, I was very much looking forward to meeting the world-renowned expert on the ancient history of the Middle East.

Mazar, a small, white-haired man then in his late seventies, answered the door, invited me into his modest apartment, and insisted on serving me a cup of coffee. As we drank our coffee, I described the sequence of events that had preceded Adam's phone call to him. I could tell that I was communicating my excitement. He excused himself from the table and hastened to prepare for our trip to the West Bank excavation.

Within moments we were out on the street and about to climb into the van, but just as I opened the door, he stopped. He told me that he'd have to run back to his apartment because he had forgotten to bring his Bible. I said that he would be able to use any of a wide selection of Bibles that we had back at the site. "Not like this one," he assured me and hurried back into the building. I waited at the curb, wondering what would be so special about the Bible he would bring.

A few minutes later, he emerged from the building, and I saw that he was carrying a small, black-plastic-covered volume. To me, it looked just like the Bibles Israeli school children use for their compulsory Bible study. Why, I wondered, had Mazar felt it necessary to make a special trip for such a commonplace edition: the tiny print was difficult to read and there was no commentary.

Responding to my obvious bewilderment, Mazar opened the book and showed me the hand-written dedication on the inside of the front cover. The book had been a gift from his deceased brother-in-law, Yitzhak Ben Zvi. Ben Zvi, a man much beloved, respected, and known for his modesty as well as for his scholarship, had been the second president of the State of Israel. Mazar lived across the street from the Ben Zvi Institute, a research center dedicated to the study and promulgation of the history of the land and the people of Israel. He told me that since the day he'd received that gift from Ben Zvi, he'd never visited an archaeological site in Israel without carrying that Bible.

Driving toward Mount Ebal, we made our way north of Jerusalem past Mount Scopus, where the new campus of the Hebrew University had been built after the Six-Day War. The mountain was the site of the original university campus, which had been there since 1929, but when Jordan captured the surrounding areas during the

War of Independence, Israel had had to establish a second campus in the Israeli sector of Jerusalem. The mountain had remained an Israeli enclave within Jordanian territory, but the armistice agreements allowed regular units of Israeli soldiers, dressed as policemen, to patrol the area for the 19 years it remained in Jordanian hands.

As we traveled along the winding road, Mazar reminisced about the recent and ancient past of the places we were passing. I realized that it had been some time since he'd last traveled that road and that he was immensely pleased to be back. In that one short hour, he taught me an entire course on the history of the places along the road. But the historical, biblical, and geographic gems Mazar shared with me were only a small part of what he taught me that morning. In my excitement to tell Mazar all about what we had found at the Ebal site, I exclaimed, "Professor, isn't it wonderful? We can actually prove the validity of the Bible!" I shall always remember his sobering response: "My young friend," he intoned, "we don't have to prove the Bible. We have to understand it."

That morning was the first of many times I met with Mazar. He helped me learn how to channel my enthusiasm and interest into an organized search for understanding of the Bible, or at least parts of it. Today, more than 20 years later, I wouldn't even think of saying that I have come close to mastering the subject. I take some consolation in the fact that I have learned that nobody else can make that claim either.

When we drove up to the site, Adam greeted Mazar with a warm embrace. I could see that their relationship transcended the usual teacher-pupil relationship. Mazar was visibly excited about all Adam and I had told him, but even in his excitement, he was a professional. He would reserve judgment until the completion of more extensive investigations and research.

As I was driving Mazar back from Ebal to Jerusalem, I suggested that we stop at Shiloh, where another of his students, Israel Finkelstein, was conducting an excavation. Mazar wholeheartedly agreed, and I turned left at the signpost reading Shiloh, about 20 miles south of our excavation.

Shiloh, famous as the Israelite sanctuary where the prophet Samuel was raised as a child and as the home of the Ark of the Covenant before its capture by the Philistines, has been excavated a number of times since 1926, when a Danish expedition first dug there. The location of ancient Shiloh has been remembered throughout history, especially because of the nearby Arab town that retains the name. Gush Emunim had established a town in the hills overlooking Shiloh, making Finkelstein's excavation logistically convenient.

Finkelstein, whom I had met once before, was pleasantly surprised by our visit. That very day, he had unearthed a small idol of the Canaanite Late Bronze period. Finkelstein passed it to Mazar for his judgment. Mazar, in turn, handed the delicately carved piece to me, stating that my opinion was certainly as good as his. I was amazed at the great scholar's modest refusal to flaunt his knowledge and wisdom.

The idea that I would be able to identify the carving as easily as Mazar was, of course, preposterous. But Mazar explained what he meant: "My opinion is too jaded," he said. "I have seen hundreds of statuettes, and I am more than likely to base my opinion on something I have seen before. You, on the other hand, have little experience, but you have a good mind. I really want to hear your opinion because it is unbiased." Even with my lack of experience, I felt confident saying that the figurine was likely a depiction of Astarte, the Canaanite fertility goddess.

Mazar's comment would come back to me as our work progressed. I realized that no one joins the study of ancient Israelite and biblical history without bringing some preconceived notions. All biblical researchers have grown up within certain environments, and each environment implies certain attitudes that color subsequent interpretation of evidence.

In the introduction to his wonderful book about current biblical theories, *Who Wrote the Bible?*, Dr. Richard Elliot Friedman, a Harvard-educated professor at Stanford University, describes the criteria that define biblical scholarship. He includes objectivity, but I maintain that objectivity is virtually impossible for students of the Bible. One cannot live in the Western world without developing some deep-seated notions about the Bible. This, I believe, is a fact. Period.

Since the day I met Mazar, I have tried diligently to develop an opinion and an attitude that supersede my own prejudices and preconceived notions. Honestly, I will not claim to have succeeded, but I have made a conscious effort in that direction.

At the end of the day, when I pulled the van up to the curb in front of Mazar's home in Jerusalem, he invited me in for a drink, and I gratefully accepted his offer. Once we were seated in his small book-lined study, I turned to him and asked, "How can I learn more?" In retrospect, I think that he must have been amused by my enthusiasm, but he was much too gracious to let me know that.

Mazar looked at me for a moment, and then he told me that he thought it was critical that the study of the Ebal site be conducted as an interdisciplinary exercise. The increasingly specialized nature of academic study—and archaeology was no exception—was slicing the perspective of research into paper-thin categories. Because of the ever-narrowing range of researchers' expertise and interest, discoveries with broad implications were almost inevitably neglected.

And thus Mazar launched me into the next phase of my Ebal journey: an interdisciplinary search for the keys that would unlock the full significance of our discovery. The Ebal site certainly provided plenty of subject matter that could be examined from the perspectives of many different disciplines. I would need to find my way through mountains of books and articles relating to cultic sites, the historical period, literary devices in the biblical text, geographic and ecological issues, and even political considerations of yesteryear.

I take credit for one insight: recognizing the vastness of the task before me. In 1987 Adam had a little party to celebrate ten years of the survey. Most of the members of what we all thought of as Adam's "inner circle" were there, and he asked each of us to say a few words. When it was my turn, I said, "It will take longer than our lifetimes to fully realize and understand all the implications of Ebal." Of course, today I realize how much of an understatement that was.

*   *   *

After meeting Mazar, I resolved to be more organized and more serious in my efforts to do research related to our discovery. Deciding to start with a review of traditional Jewish sources before tackling the scholarly and scientific ones, I turned first to the mother of all traditional sources, the Bible itself. Ebal is mentioned twice in Deuteronomy, but only the second mention refers specifically to the altar. I started with that chapter:

²It shall be on the day you cross the Jordan to the land that the Lord, your God gives you, you shall set up great stones and you shall coat them with plaster. 3 You shall inscribe on them all the words of this Torah....⁴...you shall erect these stones, of which I command you this day, in Mount Ebal, and you shall coat them with plaster. ⁵ There you shall build an altar to the Lord, your God, an altar of stones; you shall not raise iron upon them. ⁶Of whole stones shall you build the altar of the Lord, your God.... ⁸ You shall inscribe on the stones all of the words of this Torah, well clarified. (Deuteronomy 27:2-8.)

These verses are opaque at best. Certainly their meaning is not easily accessible. Deuteronomy 27:2 calls for setting up stones upon crossing the Jordan, 40 miles east of Ebal. Do these stones have something to do with Ebal? Could it be that the Israelites dragged stones for 40 miles and at the end of that trek, to make an altar, they pushed them up to the top of a 2,700-foot mountain? That seems highly unlikely. After all, the stones of the altar that we found match the stones that are native to Ebal.

For now, 27:2 remains a mystery.

Even Deuteronomy 27:4, which does mention Mount Ebal, is not clear about whether the stones that were to be set up and plastered were the same stones that were to be used for the altar mentioned in 27:5. Furthermore, it remains unclear whether those stones were the stones cited in 27:8, the stones upon which the Torah should be written.

The entire situation becomes even more complicated when the verses in Deuteronomy are compared with the relevant verses from the book of Joshua: *³⁰ Then Joshua built an altar to the Lord, God of Israel, in Mount Ebal, ³¹as Moses, servant of the Lord, had commanded the children of Israel, as it is written in the book of the Torah of Moses—an altar of whole stones.... ³² He inscribed there, on the stones, a repetition of the Torah of Moses....* (Joshua 8:30-32.)

These verses from Joshua indicate that the law was written on the stones of the altar. So why is the text in Deuteronomy unclear on this point?

To most people, such questions seem silly. Who cares? Why would anyone get worked up about the meaning of ancient texts that describe a ceremony that was to have taken place thousands of years ago, a ceremony that invokes such arcana as blessings, curses, animal sacrifices, and altars covered with plaster?

My response is that our understanding of those texts may be a key to unlocking mysteries of Western monotheism. The caterpillar of biblical analysis may metamorphose into the butterfly of understanding.

Before reviewing the text of the first Ebal reference in Deuteronomy, I made a pass through the next layer of traditional sources, the Talmud. The Talmud comprises the Mishnah, which is mentioned above (you'll remember the book with the drawing of the altar) and the Gemara, which consists primarily of commentary on the Mishnah.

Let me present some additional background about the Mishnah: it has six parts, each of which covers a different category of Jewish law. The editor of the Mishnah, Judah the Prince, was the leader of the Jewish community at about 200 CE, one of the more successful eras of the Roman Empire. Rome ruled Israel, and its emperor, Septimus Severus, was a benevolent leader. Judah and he were known to have been close friends.

The 150 years that preceded the reign of Septimus Severus had been a period of terrible turmoil and destruction for the Jews of Israel. Titus, son of Vespasian, had destroyed the Second Temple in 70 CE. The best-known reference to that event is still visible in the Forum near the Coliseum in Rome. The Arch of Titus depicts Roman soldiers triumphantly marching from the Temple, carrying off such valuables as its Menorah, a huge golden candelabrum.

Forty years later, between 114 CE and 117 CE, Jews from outside Israel, in other parts of the Empire, revolted against Rome, and their uprising was brutally crushed. The Jews of Israel suffered a devastating catastrophe between 132 CE and 135 CE when, under the leadership of Bar Kokhba, they again rebelled against Roman rule. The Talmud describes the slaughter in graphic detail, lamenting that on the battlefield at Betar, which is located about five miles south of Jerusalem, the blood of the slain Jews ran so deep that it reached the nostrils of the Roman horses. But from a spiritual point of view, the most ruinous aspect of the revolt was that many Jews had believed that Bar Kokhba was the Messiah. Among those believers was Rabbi Akiva, the foremost scholar of his generation.

Hadrian, the emperor, was so infuriated by the rebellion that he took retaliatory steps whose profound effects are felt even today. He ordered the torture of the ten most respected Jewish scholars. The liturgy of Yom Kippur, the Day of Atonement, recalls their deaths in bone-chilling detail.

The emperor denied all Jews entrance to Jerusalem, particularly to the ruins of the destroyed Temple. And in a vicious attempt to eradicate the Jewish relationship with Jerusalem and Israel, Hadrian changed the name of Jerusalem to Ilia Capitolina. He then built a new city at Shechem, just beneath Mount Ebal, and named it Neapolis. Neapolis, which literally means "new city," still exists as an Arab city. But because Arabic does not have a "P" equivalent, over time, the city's name evolved, and the city is now known as Nablus.

Yasser Arafat and the Palestinians owe Hadrian a huge debt, for it was he who gave Israel a new name: Palestine. (Ironically, because Arabic lacks a "P" equivalent, Arabs can't pronounce "Palestine" correctly.) Hadrian derived that name from a biblical tribe, the Philistines, who arrived on the Mediterranean shores of Canaan from Greek and other islands at about the same time the Israelites were crossing the Jordan River and entering the land. Initially, the Philistines were a formidable enemy who bore down hard on the Israelites with sophisticated and superior weaponry. After several centuries of struggle, however, the Israelites overcame the Philistines, who left few historical traces after the time of King David. According to some historians, the Philistines moved north, settling mainly in what is today Lebanon, and they became the Phoenician nation.

It is quite clear that there were no Philistines in the land when Hadrian, more than 1,000 years after their disappearance, decided to revive their name. Strangely enough, no nation elected to claim the Palestinian name until 1,790 years later, when in 1926, Haj Amin Al Husseini, Grand Mufti of Jerusalem, reinvented the term and lay claim to the land on behalf of "Palestinian" Arabs.

Although there were peaceful relations with Rome during the reign of Septimus, the Jewish community, which was forbidden to rebuild Jerusalem, was centered in the Galilee, at Zippori. Reviewing history, Judah, a practical and brilliant man, realized that it wouldn't take much to destroy the Jewish nation entirely. He took advantage of the relatively calm political atmosphere to create a law code that would bind Jews to their religious tradition. He reasoned that in the event of another exile or any other national catastrophe, this code of laws would guard the identity of the Jewish community. It was this goal that prompted Judah's collation of the Mishnah.

Judah's plan was enormously effective. Until the modern era, almost all Jews felt bound to Jewish law, the basis of which was the Mishnah. Jewish tradition describes the Mishnah as the first part of the Oral Law. (The Written Law is, of course, the Torah.) Tradition has it that the Oral Law, the correct interpretation of Torah, originated at Sinai and was passed from generation to generation, finding written form in its codification in the Mishnah.

*   *   *

Back to Ebal: In the Mishnah and the Talmud, I found only one brief review of the story of the blessings and curses. That reference appears in *Sotah,* a rather neglected tractate. Perhaps its name has something to do with the relative lack of attention paid to this tractate. *Sotah* refers to the ordeal faced by the suspected wife of a jealous husband. To determine whether or not she is guilty of adultery, the wife must drink a terrible concoction made by the priests. Survival—an unlikely possibility—is the only acceptable proof of the woman's innocence. Most religious-school teachers find that explaining the concept of adultery to young, sheltered Orthodox children is a loathsome task, and that may account for this tractate's lack of popularity.

It is not widely known that even according to the strictest interpretation, Jews may recite almost the entire prayer service in any language, not necessarily in Hebrew. The seventh chapter of tractate *Sotah, Ela Ne'emarin,* means literally "those that are spoken." The Mishnah in that chapter lists those texts that must be recited in Hebrew only, as well as those that may be recited in any language. Deuteronomy 27:15-26 the verses that contain blessings and curses are among the few texts that must be recited in Hebrew.

Let us consider the Mishnah's description of that part of the ceremony of the blessings and the curses that is relevant to the altar:

And then [after reciting the blessings and the curses], *they brought the stones and built the altar and plastered it with plaster and wrote upon it all the words of the Torah in 70 languages...and then took the stones to their camp.* (Talmud Sotah, page 32:1 and 2.)

Apparently, the Mishnah has a simple resolution for the problem of the stones. It accepts the text from Joshua: the writing was done in plaster on the stones of the altar. The Mishnah ignores the biblical text's problematic suggestion that there might have been more than one set of stones.

On what basis does the Mishnah determine that it was written in 70 languages? *You shall inscribe on the stones all of the words of this Torah, well clarified.* (Deuteronomy 27:8.) According to Jewish tradition, every word of God's Bible has meaning; and "well clarified," the rabbis argued, must mean that anyone who would see the inscription would understand it. That 70 languages would be a comprehensive total of all human languages is understood from the biblical narrative that describes God's destruction of the Tower of Babel in Genesis 11. Tradition holds that the peoples were scattered into 70 nations, each with its own language.

In our excavations, we found no inscriptions, not even in Hebrew, much less in 70 languages. But I am confident that originally there must have been inscriptions at the site. Here's why:

As I've already mentioned, two walls surround the altar. The first wall encompasses the immediate area, creating an enclosure of about one acre. The second encloses a much larger area, about three and one-half acres. Adam defined the inner area as a *temenos,* a Greek term that describes an enclosure of a sacred site.

One day in the course of our 1985 excavations, as I was strolling along the eastern corner of the outer perimeter, my attention was caught by a formation of stones beneath the underbrush. When I cleared away the brush, I was startled to see a complete circle of stones, with a white rim along the bottom and the inside of the circle. As I continued to clear away the brush within the circle, the white rim turned into a white side wall of a stone pit that was emerging gradually. Immediately, I summoned one of the archaeologists, and he, upon seeing what I'd found, ran off to fetch Adam.

It turns out that I had uncovered a pit that had been used to mix plaster. That same season, digging inside the altar, we found 20 plaster slabs that were on average six inches long, four inches wide, and one inch thick. During the period directly following the period of the altar, plaster pits had been used to hold water. But it was clear that "my" pit had been built for the purpose of mixing plaster.

Our excavations of the site have yet to yield a single inscription on plaster. Nevertheless, we remain confident that the plaster at the site must have been for use in inscriptions, a fairly common usage in the ancient Middle East. Perhaps the heavy rainfall on Mount Ebal has eroded the ancient inscriptions or—and this is really exciting—those tablets may still be buried, awaiting discovery.

According to the Mishnah, once the blessings and curses ceremony had been completed, the Israelites gathered the stones and took them to their camp. The pottery from our dig indicates that the Mount Ebal site was active for 70 to 100 years, and it was certainly not a one-shot deal. Although the Mishnaic interpretation implies that the altar was only a temporary entity, our excavations indicate quite clearly that this was not so.

We are also puzzled by the Mishnah's reference to "their camp." It can refer only to the site known as Gilgal, which in Joshua is described as being in the vicinity of Jericho—at least 60 miles southeast of Ebal. I give my ancestors a lot of credit for writing law codes and creating monotheism, but the Mishnah's interpretation that the Israelites dragged immense stones across 60 miles is beyond credibility. What, then, is the answer to the camp question?

As part of the instructions regarding the other biblical mention of the blessings and curses in Deuteronomy, the text in Deuteronomy 11 presents a five-part, Baedeker-like series of instructions that detail the approach to Mount Ebal:

> [26] *See, I present before you today a blessing and a curse....* [29] *It shall be that when the Lord, your God, brings you to the land to which you come to possess it, then you shall deliver the blessing on Mount Gerizim and the curse on Mount Ebal.* [30] *Are they not on the other side of the Jordan, far, in the direction of the sunset, in the land of the Canaanite, that dwells in the plain, opposite the Gilgal, near Elonei Moreh?* (Deuteronomy 11:26-30.)

Deuteronomy describes the Israelites' wandering in the Moabite plains east of the Jordan River. It's clear, therefore, that the first leg of their journey to Shechem must take them across the Jordan. Step one of the travel directions, the other side of the Jordan, is easily understandable.

Next, they are to travel in the direction of the setting sun. With the Jordan River lying east of Shechem, standing on the banks of the river, one can see the sun set and sink slowly behind Mount Gerizim and Mount Ebal.

The Canaanite plain, the Aravah, is associated with the low-lying flat area that flanks the Jordan on both sides, stretching from the southern end of the Sea of Galilee, all the way to the Red Sea. It makes sense that the Israelites would cross that low plain to reach Shechem.

The fourth indicator, opposite the Gilgal, presents a geographic problem. As I've mentioned, the book of Joshua tells us that the Gilgal is the Israelites' camp near Jericho, fifty or so miles to the southeast. Can the site of the ceremony be "opposite" this Gilgal? It does not make sense that they would be camped so far away; it seems incomprehensible and certainly impossible that the Gilgal referred to in this verse is near Jericho.

Over the years, rabbis who studied this text also contended with the difficulties this passage presents, and they went to excruciating lengths to explain that there is no problematic discrepancy. Rabbi Eliezer, a commentator quoted in the Jerusalem Talmud, suggests that two small mounds near Jericho had been designated as Gerizim and Ebal, and the ceremony of the blessings and the curses was, in fact, conducted there rather than in the vicinity of Shechem. This is farfetched: the location of Gerizim and Ebal in the vicinity of Shechem is absolutely indisputable.

Rashi, perhaps the most respected rabbinical commentator, also went out on a limb. He wrote that the Hebrew word *mool,* which ordinarily means "opposite," has a different meaning in this sentence, and he translates it as "far from" the Gilgal. I don't buy that. What is far, however, is the distance between Rashi's interpretation in this case and his usually sound logic.

One day, during the 1985 season, just as we had finished eating lunch at our Shavei Shomron campsite, Adam presented a solution that does make sense to me. He invited me along with Judy Dekel, the talented artist who drew most of Adam's archaeological renderings, to join him on an excursion. The three of us climbed into the jeep and headed east toward Shechem. Rather than taking the turn that would lead us to our excavation, we continued past Joseph's Tomb through the city of Nablus and took the road east towards the Jordan Valley.

About three miles past Nablus, we turned onto a dirt path, passing a few isolated Arab homes. We followed the path for about half a mile, until it simply stopped at what appeared to be a poorly maintained stone wall. Approaching a breach in the wall, we could see that it enclosed a fairly large area—about ten acres. The northern edge of the expanse reached the Tirza River, a river whose waters originate in the mountains and flow into the Jordan. The mountains tower over the valley, and in less than two miles, the ground elevation drops more than 2,000 feet.

Even in the heat of summer, the perennial water flow of the Tirza creates an oasis in this otherwise arid area, so the valley is always lush and green, studded with banana, orange, lemon, and tangerine trees, as well as rich vegetable patches and wheat fields. As I gazed at the sight before me, I marveled that the Song of Songs is absolutely brilliant in its comparison of the Tirza with a beautiful woman.

Adam led us to a spot on the southern part of the enclosure where we saw an arrangement of stones that extended aboveground for about two feet. Lifting his arm, he directed our attention to the east, towards Ebal. Both Judy and I were amazed that standing there, we were able to make out the site of our excavations. Capitalizing on our surprise, Adam announced, "You are now at the Gilgal, opposite Ebal."

Adam, who in his younger years penned and published a volume of poetry, has a definite flair for the dramatic. I thought that I was already accustomed to his penchant for trying to astonish us, but that day, he certainly caught me off my guard.

He explained that although it appeared that we were looking at an uneven stone wall, it was actually a wall made of piles of stones. The Hebrew word *gal*, part of the word Gilgal, means pile, usually of stones. Adam believes that the biblical reference to Gilgal does not point to a particular geographic location. Rather, he says, it is describing a type of place, denoted by a wall made of piles of stones. A few years later, in fact, Adam unearthed a similar formation near the Jordan. Finkelstein, in his survey of the territory of Ephraim, found two more similar structures. Each of those two structures conforms to a different biblical reference to Gilgal.

I cherish the memory of Adam's satisfaction at our wonder. It seemed miraculous to stand at Gilgal, repeating the biblical text and actually seeing the geographic progression from east to west, exactly as it is presented in Deuteronomy. But that was not the end of Adam's surprise.

The fifth step of the biblical travel instructions reads, "next to Elonei Moreh." Where should we be looking for Elonei Moreh, and what is its significance?

There is only one other biblical reference to this place. *Abram passed into the land as far as the site of Shechem, until Elon Moreh.* (Genesis 12:6.) Early in his journey from his Mesopotamian homeland, and before God changed his name to Abraham, Abram stopped in Elon Moreh. It was his first stop in the Promised Land. He built an altar at Elon Moreh, and according to the very next verse, God appeared to him there, pronouncing the words that form the entire and sole foundation of Zionism and Jewish claims to the land of Israel: *To your offspring I will give this land.* (Genesis 12:7.)

The travel instructions in Deuteronomy 11:30 direct the Israelites' attention in a progression from east to west. If the fourth indicator was this Gilgal, then Elonei Moreh should in turn be located to the west of it; east of and, as the text says, "next to" Ebal.

There is only one location in the vicinity that fits those particulars. We left Gilgal and headed west towards Nablus, the site of biblical Shechem. But instead of making a right turn towards Shavei Shomron, we made a left and drove to a hilltop known in Arabic as Jebel Kabir, the "great mountain." One of the peaks of Jebel Kabir is the site of the tomb of Sheikh Bil'al. Bil'al was the muezzin—the crier who the calls Moslem faithful to prayer—of the prophet Muhammad.

Until recently, traditional Arabs believed that Bil'al was buried at this site, and they visited the site on Moslem religious holidays. But about a century ago, certain scholars of Islam proved that Bil'al had died in what is now Iraq and that he was buried there. Since then, this site's importance to Moslems has dissipated.

However, the very same spot atop the peak of Jebel Kabir is quite possibly the site of Elon Moreh. What is the basis of that assertion?

First, in confirmation of the biblical description, the peak of Jebel Kabir is the only notable geographic entity between Gilgal and Ebal.

Second, it is widely known that the holy sites of Islam in the land of Israel are almost always built on sites that had been holy to earlier cultures. The most obvious example of this practice is Jerusalem's famed Dome of the Rock, which according to most traditions, is built directly above the ruins of the Holy of Holies of the Second Temple. It is likely, therefore, that the peak of Jebel Kabir was regarded as a holy place long before it was designated as the sheikh's burial spot.

Third, the Moslems named this hilltop Jebel Kabir, "great mountain," even though both nearby Ebal and Gerizim are taller. We conjecture that the "greatness" refers to the location's connection with the great Abram (later Abraham), patriarch of Moslems as well as Jews.

Fourth, oak trees flourish on this mountaintop. Botanists have advised us that if oaks are growing there today, then they were there during the time of the patriarchs. In Genesis, the Plain of Moreh is called Elon Moreh and in Deuteronomy, it is called Elonai Moreh. *Elon* is the Hebrew word for "oak" and *elonei* is a plural form of elon.

Fifth, *moreh,* the second half of that name, is derived from a Hebrew word that means "to teach" or "to show." The narrative tells us that God promised Abram the land—the land that was visible from where he was standing. In other words, God is showing Abram the Promised Land. In this case, it seems, "show" is the meaning of the name Moreh.

There is no better place from which to view the land of Israel. Despite the scourge of air pollution that contaminates even the sparsely industrialized West Bank, a person standing on that peak can see Jerusalem to the south, almost the entire coastal plain to the west, a good part of the Galilee to the north, and all of Transjordan that was inhabited by the ancient Israelites to the east.

Admittedly, none of those guesses can be proven "scientifically." But a sixth reason presents a most compelling argument for drawing a connection between Elon Moreh and Jebel Kabir.

A temenos—a wall that surrounds a holy place—encircles the gravesite. And on the basis of evidence from the pottery shards that have been found along the wall, that wall has been dated to the second part of the Middle Bronze Era, or

MB2. MB2, according to such an esteemed archaeologist as Albright, is the period of the patriarchs.

Furthermore, at the site, archaeologists have found a continuity of pottery that extends throughout the Iron Age, when the Israelites controlled the area. This means that, although the hilltop was not inhabited, it was visited regularly by the Israelites. It's reasonable to assume that those visits were motivated by the historic importance of the hilltop.

This discovery is rather sensational in itself. But an event that occurred only 30 years ago makes it all the more astonishing.

Among the first Gush Emunim settlers in Samaria was the Elon More group, which in 1977 settled near an Arab town called Rujeib, south of Nablus. Arab landowners protested that some of the lands the Israeli government had confiscated were their own private lands. Those Arabs took their case to court and won. (A few years later, it turned out that their claims to the land had been supported by false documentation.)

Subsequently, in 1981 Ariel Sharon, then Israel's Minister of Agriculture, faced a pressing problem. Being in charge of the Jewish settlements in the West Bank and Gaza, he was responsible for the evacuation of the Elon More group from Rujeib. The Israeli Supreme Court had given him only a few weeks to locate an alternate site that would also be acceptable to the group.

When his search for public lands in the vicinity of Nablus ended with the choice of Jebel Kabir, Israeli Air Force helicopters airlifted the settlers' prefabricated shacks and transplanted them there. As a result of chance and the whims of the Supreme Court of Israel, the Elon More group of Gush Emunim ended up in what we believe is the original location of the biblical site of Elon Moreh, from which the group had taken its name.

Adam has been accused of politicizing the Ebal excavation and kowtowing to Gush Emunim. I, however, don't think such criticism is merited. If there were even a kernel of truth to it, Gush Emunim would have been quick to take Adam's hypothesis and milk it for political and psychological advantage. The story meshes perfectly with the settlers' messianic ideas and political philosophy. It seems almost too good to be true: Ariel Sharon, one of the few politicians whom members of Gush Emunim respect, actually led a group that calls itself Elon More to what we believe was the Elon Moreh from which Abram viewed the land of Israel for the first time.

*   *   *

As I proceeded to use the geographic "expertise" of the Talmud to analyze the biblical texts that related to the stones, I found myself asking a most troubling theological question. If the Oral Law is the correct interpretation of the Bible, why does it provide incorrect details of the ceremony of the blessings and the curses? Even for obscure biblical passages, I, as an Orthodox Jew, expected the Talmudic texts to deal with the problems with absolute divine precision.

This, however, I found was not the case. I believe that our work provides clear and irrefutable proof that the Oral Law, which at least in this case, is inconsistent with the physical evidence, is fallible and therefore cannot be divine. The discrepancies between our discoveries and the traditional Jewish interpretation were enough to alienate me from the conventional Orthodox way of thought and belief. This estrangement from my spiritual core was no small matter. Not only had I raised my three children to believe in Orthodox Judaism, I was also living in a community that considered itself the spearhead of Orthodox Jewry.

Finding that traditional religious interpretation could contribute little to understanding what actually happened at the ceremony of the blessings and curses, I undertook a study of the academic and scientific sources. There, too, I found huge gaps and discrepancies to contend with.

Although the traditional belief is that Moses himself wrote the Pentateuch, various commentators, even such Orthodox commentators as Ibn Ezra of 14th century Spain, have found problems with this view. The book of Deuteronomy opens as follows: *These are the words that Moses spoke to all Israel, on the other side of the Jordan.* Ibn Ezra pointed out that being on the other side of the Jordan has meaning only to people who are already within the borders of Israel. Still, the Bible reports that Moses never crossed the Jordan into Israel. Rather, he died on Mount Nebo, where he had inscribed the entire book of Deuteronomy. It seems clear that such a sentence must have been written by someone within the land of Israel, west of the Jordan. Ibn Ezra notes that anyone who understands that there is a problem here should remain silent about it.

That is only one of a plethora of textual challenges to Mosaic authorship of the Pentateuch. In Genesis 36, for example, a list of Edomite kings that presumably reigned during the patriarchal period includes the names of rulers who lived no fewer than 500 years after Moses.

Most of us are familiar with other literary and logical inconsistencies in the biblical narrative. The verses that tell us about Noah seem to offer two versions of the flood story. Perhaps there was an editor who, having to contend with the two versions, made a valiant attempt to combine them.

One need look no further than the opening verses of the Bible. The story of Creation, like the story of Noah, seems to comprise two distinct threads. God's creation of man, for example is described first: *²⁶And God said, "Let us make man in Our image...." ²⁷So God created man in His image, in the image of God He created him: male and female He created them.* (Genesis 1:26-27.)

In those verses, the first version, God, *Elohim,* creates both man and woman. The creation of woman, in this version, was simultaneous with the creation of man.

Several verses later, we find a narrative that tells a different story of man's creation: *⁷And the Lord God formed the man of dust from the ground, and He blew into his nostrils the soul of life; and man became a living being....*(Genesis 2:7.) In this version, the Lord, *Adonai,* creates man alone, not in the image of God, but from the earth. Woman doesn't appear for several verses: *²¹So the Lord God cast a deep sleep upon the man and he slept; and He took one of his ribs and He filled in flesh in its place. ²²Then the Lord God fashioned the rib that He had taken from the man into a woman, and He brought her to the man.* (Genesis 2:21-22.)

As a result of the two apparently different versions, scholars have identified two different sources—different authorship originating in different eras.

Mainstream biblical scholarship promoted by Julius Wellhausen, a 19th century German Semitist, has identified no fewer than four distinct Old Testament "sources." Wellhausen dubbed them J (biblical texts that use YHVH—Jehovah—as the name of God), E (those passages that refer to God as Elohim), D (Deuteronomy and related texts in Joshua, Judges, and Kings), and P (Priestly Code in Leviticus and parts of Exodus and Numbers). Of course, even scholars who subscribe to the theory that the biblical text was authored by several different sources disagree about attribution of certain verses and even chapters. Furthermore, it is acknowledged that the big four—J, E, D, and P—themselves have been edited many times over the years, and they are usually subdivided to represent a number of secondary authors. The scrolls, after all, were hand-copied by humans who labored for countless hours, introducing subtle—and generally inadvertent—variations to the texts.

The E source is said to have been authored in Northern Israel during the tenth century BCE and the J source is thought to have been written in Judah during the eighth century BCE. The entire book of Leviticus and the parts of Exodus and Numbers that deal with priestly matters are believed to have been written by the P source, which Wellhausen dates to the Second Temple period, only a few centuries before Christianity.

The D source is associated mainly with Deuteronomy, and its distinctly poetic style uses phraseology not seen in the other sources. In particular, D deals with the Temple, calling it "the Place that He will choose." That phrase appears 34 times in Deuteronomy but nowhere else in the Pentateuch. Traditional Judaism maintains that any reference to the Temple in Deuteronomy was the prophecy of Moses, relating to the temple built by Solomon in Jerusalem, some 300 years later. Scientific investigators view Deuteronomy, which focuses on what is known as the Centralization of the Cult, as ex post facto text—text that was written after the fact.

Centralization of the Cult was first proposed in 1805 by Wilhelm Martin Leberecht De Wette, a German biblical scholar and theologian. His work calls attention to the uniqueness of Deuteronomy and its concentration on cultic activities, including sacrifice, that may take place only at "the Place that He will choose," the place designated by God as the location for the Temple.

According to De Wette, a quick search in the Bible reveals a particular point in history when the concept of Centralization of the Cult was born. The later chapters of the book of Kings II (Kings II: 22-23) tell the story of King Josiah, a righteous and pious king. During Josiah's reign, the high priest, Hilkiya, discovered a long-lost scroll in the Temple. He took it to the scribe Shaphan, who presented it to the king. Upon reading the scroll, the king rent his clothes, a sign of mourning among Jews to this day, and set out to, among other things, destroy all the places of cultic activity located outside Jerusalem. This effectively centralized all cultic activity in his capital. An earlier king, Hizkiyahu, had also done away with cultic sites outside Jerusalem, but unlike Josiah, he did not act as a result of having read a specific scroll.

De Wette put two and two together, and came up with the idea that because Centralization is mentioned only in Deuteronomy, Deuteronomy must be a product of the period of Josiah, and a *pia fraua*—a pious fraud—written later and artificially put into the mouth of Moses.

Josiah, like any astute political leader, wanted Jerusalem, his capital, to be the exclusive location of cultic activity. De Wette theorizes that Josiah instructed his scribes to write Deuteronomy as if the words had come directly from the mouth of Moses.

The Deuteronomic text imparted stature, power, and economic strength to Josiah. For example, Deuteronomy states that all males are obligated to bring sacrifices to the chosen place three times annually. In modern times, such a requirement would translate into enormous profits for a government that owns, say, the local Holiday Inn, the sole slaughterhouse, and the only Coca-Cola concession in town. It could sell soft drinks at one gate, draft people into the army at another, collect back taxes at all the gates, and, in general, strengthen its hold on the nation.

Although modern scholarship has refined De Wette's analysis of Deuteronomy, identifying at least five secondary sources, his understanding of Centralization remains the scholarly standard. In particular, his dating of Deuteronomy to the end of the seventh century BCE, the period of Josiah, is now considered fundamental. In his book, *Introduction to Deuteronomy*, Dr. Alexander Rofe of the Hebrew University synopsizes the currently accepted view that the entire system of dating other biblical sources is based on their relationship to source D, whose dating is considered to be the soundest.

So both the traditional and scientific views coincide here and unequivocally identify "the Place that He will choose" as the Temple site in Jerusalem.

The Ebal episode presents a puzzling problem for this accepted view. Remember: this view assumes that Deuteronomy was composed no earlier than 620 BCE and that it is the product of the court of a Judean king, descended from the House of David, a monarchy that had always been centered in Jerusalem. Why then, should Deuteronomy include an episode that describes an extremely important ceremony that was to take place at Gerizim and Ebal, the two mountains above Shechem? Shechem was the first capital of the Northern Kingdom of Israel, which split from the House of David during the reign of Rehoboam, grandson of David. Shechem was chosen by Jeroboam, the rebel leader who subsequently became the first king of the Northern Kingdom of Israel, because, as a historical and cultic center of Israel, Shechem could withstand rivalry from Jerusalem. Why would the authors of Deuteronomy, during the reign of Josiah—a descendant of David, scion of Jerusalem—include it in their manuscript?

For another possible answer, let's return to the Ebal texts in Deuteronomy.

Adam had pointed out that the biblical text describes the altar as being *behar Eval,* or "in Mount Ebal." (Deuteronomy 27:4, Deuteronomy 27:13, and Joshua 8:30.) When the text mentions Mount Gerizim, it always says *al har Gerizim,* or "on Mount Gerizim." Only in Deuteronomy 11:29, the introduction to and first mention of the ceremony, does the biblical text neglect to make the distinction between Ebal and Gerizim, and uses the term *al,* or "on", for both. I have seen no English translation that makes the distinction between "in" and "on." But we viewed it as quite significant when we realized that our site is actually "in" Mount Ebal. The mountain has four slopes, and the altar site is on the third slope from the top. If the text had been referring to the top of the mountain, the verse would, or should read, "on Mount Ebal," as do the Gerizim references. If the text had been referring to the foot of the mountain, it might read *betachtit,* or "at the base," as it does when it describes the position of the Israelites at Mount Sinai. (Exodus 19:17.)

Three times the Bible described the altar site as being "in" the mountain, exactly as we found it. The meaning is clear: the text was written by someone familiar with the site. Furthermore, the author must have lived contemporaneously, at the time the site was active, circa 1200 BCE. Here's my reasoning:

The carbon-14 testing of the bones and the easily identifiable Iron I shards from our dig reveal that the site had been deliberately buried within 70 to 100 years of its having been built. De Wette's dating of Deuteronomy places its compilation near the end of the seventh century BCE, during the reign of King Josiah. If De Wette's assumptions are correct, how would the scribes of Josiah's time know to describe the site as being in Mount Ebal? After its mention in the book of Joshua, there is no further biblical reference to Mount Ebal. Certainly scribes of the Kingdom of Judah, living and writing in their holy city of Jerusalem during the reign of King Josiah, would have had little interest in promoting an important ceremony relating to Shechem, which had served as the first capital of the renegade Kingdom of Israel under Jeroboam.

As I see it, we have raised two questions for the accepted scholarly position: Why would the scribes of Josiah recount this story? How would those scribes have known that the site of the altar was "in" Mount Ebal?

Scholars have given consideration to my first question, Why did the scribes of Josiah enter this story into Deuteronomy? Their answer has been, almost unanimously, that parts of Deuteronomy are "Northern Heritage texts" that originated in the Northern Kingdom of Israel and were copied by Josiah's scribes. And what terminology do they use to describe this process? They explain that the material "seeped" into Deuteronomy.

I love this answer because it is so convoluted, so befuddling, so inappropriate—particularly in this case—and so typical of biblical scholarship's response to contradictions in the absence of legitimate, logical answers. Rather than questioning the hypothesis that places the writing of Deuteronomy in the seventh century BCE, the scholars respond to the textual conundrum as if it were a blob of muck that "seeped" into the text like a wormy, uninvited guest.

The seepage terminology is symptomatic of the attitude of biblical scholars to the historical relevance of the biblical narrative, especially the material that describes the premonarchic period, before 1000 BCE, the era of David and Solomon. Today's scholars are the most skeptical of all, many of them having developed scientific theories that invalidate the historicity of most of the biblical narrative.

This is not to say that they developed their theories willy-nilly with no logical legitimacy. My argument with them is that once they had developed those theories, they put a stranglehold on any research that might disturb their own models. I have experienced this phenomenon firsthand.

*   *   *

Once I had satisfied myself that the site of our excavations could be identified with the biblical texts describing Mount Ebal and the ceremony of the blessings and the curses, I needed to see how that fit into the broader context of the historical record.

Because according to the biblical texts, the ceremony was to have taken place with the Israelites' arrival in the land, my first challenge was to see whether the survey and the excavations conformed to existing evidence of the earliest Israelites in the land. I turned to historical research related to the fascinating story of Israel's entrance into Canaan, the Settlement Period.

Adam's doctoral thesis dealt with the Settlement Period in the tribal area of Mannaseh. The Settlement Period—covering the time the Israelites entered Canaan as a group of tribes until the monarchy was established—is among the most controversial subjects of historical biblical research. There is little dispute about the period involved—from 1300 to 1000 BCE. Also, most experts agree that by the time of King David, Israel had evolved as a national unit. The areas of contention are centered on where these people came from and how they combined into a national entity.

In their attempt to understand the settlement of Canaan by the people of Israel, scholars have developed three explanations: the Conquest Model, Peaceful Infiltration, and the Sociological Theory.

The first theory, the Conquest Model, was originally put forth by Albright. He accepted the biblical texts more or less at face value, and it was his belief that the Israelites had waged a large military campaign to conquer the land, pretty much as it is described in the book of Joshua. Yigael Yadin is in agreement with Albright's theory, which, of course, is essentially the traditional religious understanding of the conquest.

For this Conquest Model, there is at least one outstanding problem. The excavations of Jericho and Ai—both of which, according to the biblical narrative, were conquered and destroyed by Joshua—reveal signs of destruction only from a period that preceded the settlement by at least 1,000 years. The generally accepted formula that is used to explain this discrepancy is that the writer of the book of Joshua saw or knew of both sites in their ruined state and ascribed their destruction to a historical Joshua, making up a truly magnificent story that continues to titillate imaginations to this day.

The second settlement model, Peaceful Infiltration, was proposed first by Albrecht Alt, a noted 20th century German scholar. He put forth the idea that the Israelites were nomadic groups who entered the land peacefully, crossing the Jordan to find pasturelands for their flocks of sheep and cattle. Gradually, the groups coalesced into tribes that became a nation. The historical configuration of this model negates both the Exodus story and the historical legitimacy of the patriarchal narratives described in the Bible.

The Peaceful Infiltration model also presents problems. It suggests that those ancient nomads came into an unpopulated Canaan. Clearly, this is not the case. A very well-known collection of texts, the El-Amarna Letters, tells us that the region around Shechem was ruled by the firm hands of King Labaya and his sons. Although, the El-Amarna Letters predate the Settlement Period by 100 years—around 1350 BCE—they provide relevant historical background for the early years of that period. Labaya and his descendants, whom the letters describe as ruthless, cunning, and wily, would never have allowed a bunch of ragged nomads simply to occupy their territory.

Furthermore, a considerable number of archaeological tels within Israel attest to the destruction of Canaanite cities by war during this period. On the other hand, the ruins of an ancient city don't provide sure identity of its conquerors, and it's at least possible that those Canaanite cities were not destroyed by Israelites.

A third model, the Sociological Theory, describes the development of Israel as an intra-Canaanite phenomenon. According to this theory, groups of Canaanite peasants revolted against their urban kings and formed tribal associations that were the origins of a future Kingdom of Israel. This theory attempts to supplant the let-my-people-go story with a sequence of events vaguely like a modern-day social revolution. It considers the biblical narratives about the Hebrew patriarchs, the sojourn in Egypt, the Exodus, the 40-year trek through Sinai, and the conquest of Israel, and reinterprets all that text as myth that may or may not have happened to a small group of so-called proto-Israelites. Subsequently, the theory holds, the entire biblical "history" of Israel was artificially superimposed upon the group of tribes that became the nation of Israel.

Modern scientific scholars eagerly adopted this theory because it allows them to explain biblical phenomena within a familiar sociological context: rebellion against oppression and striving for egalitarianism.

How does each of the three theories match up with our discoveries at Ebal? Can any of them correctly describe the settlement process as it happened in Mannaseh?

The Conquest Model quickly runs into problems in this context. Joshua 12 lists 31 Canaanite kings of city-states that the Israelites defeated. Of those 31 cities only Tapuach, Tirza, and Hefer were in Mannaseh. None of those three was a major city. It is an absolute certainty that Shechem was the most important city between Jerusalem to the south and the Valley of Jezreel to the north. So why is Shechem not mentioned as one of Joshua's conquests? Could the Israelites settle in Mannaseh without first destroying this city which dominated the region? Excavations at Shechem show that it existed rather peacefully long into the Settlement Period. The first indications of destruction, at about 1100 BCE, are consistent with the story of Abimelech, well after the Settlement Period. (Judges 9.)

The Bible does not include Shechem on the list of destroyed cities very simply because it was not destroyed at this stage of history.

What's more, the evidence points to a positive relationship between the entering Israelites and the resident Canaanite populace of Shechem. The Israelites built an important sanctuary at Ebal, less than two miles from a Canaanite sanctuary in Shechem. The Ebal sanctuary remained active for close to a century. Clearly, the Canaanites down the hill did not object to it.

Second, despite the biblical commandments to destroy *Mazzebot,* (Deuteronomy 12:3; Exodus 34:13), the large upright stones that were the focus of cultic observance at Canaanite sanctuaries, the Israelites did no such thing at Shechem. One of these stones that was in the Canaanite temple at Shechem throughout the Settlement Period, remains visible and undisturbed to this very day.

So although the Conquest Model might work for some parts of Israel, within the confines of Manasseh, the apparent coexistence of the local Canaanites and the incoming Israelites challenges the model. Adam recognized this contradiction and suggested that the Peaceful Infiltration Model seemed the more historically accurate.

Adam's survey also provides evidence that supports the idea that the Israelites entered the land opposite Shechem, rather than, as is written in the book of Joshua, opposite Jericho. One route into the land of Israel from Transjordan follows the

Far'ah and Malich *wadis,* Arabic for "riverbeds." That route leads to Shechem in Mannaseh. Archaeological excavations have revealed at least ten times as many early Settlement Period sites in Manasseh as in Ephraim and Benjamin in the southern region that includes Jericho, the traditionally accepted point-of-entry into Canaan.

There are biblical indications as well that the Israelites entered opposite Shechem. According to Deuteronomy 27:2, Moses instructed the Israelites to conduct the ceremony of blessings and curses "on the day that you cross the Jordan." "The day" need not be interpreted as exactly the day they crossed the river. Nevertheless, it must mean that the ceremony of the blessings and curses should have been performed as soon as possible after the Israelites entered the land. The verse described above, Deuteronomy 11:29, which details the route to Shechem via the Gilgal and Elonei Moreh, also describes entry to the land opposite Shechem and matches Adam's survey exactly.

That the entry point for the tribes was opposite Shechem, is also consistent with biblical indications that the area of Shechem—the region associated with the tribe of Menasseh—was the assembly point for the nation of Israel. The biblical narrative describes the activities of several other tribes in that region. There was the aggressive response of the tribes of Simeon and Levi to the rape of their sister Dinah by the Prince of Shechem. (Genesis 34.) Of course, Mannaseh and Ephraim, the sons of Joseph, were in the region during the period of Joshua, who tells his own tribe of Ephraim to go south and clear the wooded areas, to make more room for themselves. (Joshua 17:14-18.) It is possible to understand that the tribe of Asher, too, resided in this area. The Hebrew word *asher,* "which is," can be interpreted here to mean the tribe Asher (Joshua 17:7). Further evidence of Asher's presence may be understood from the name of the Arab village of Tayasir, northeast of Shechem. Its name preserves the name Asher in its Arabic form. And the first chapter of the book of Judges describes successful attacks by Judah and Simeon on the Canaanites and the Perizzites. So no fewer than 6 of the 12 tribes of Israel receive some mention as having been active in the area of Mannaseh during the pre-monarchic period. And this supports the assumption that Israelite tribes entered Canaan in this area and proceeded on their separate ways from there.

I did find at least one other clue that might shed light on the apparently good relationship between the Canaanites in Shechem and the Israelites. Back in March

1985, my town hosted a group of Hebrew University alumni who were visiting the region. Their tour was led by Y. Kiehl, a brilliant biblical expert and the editor-in-chief of *Da'at Mikra,* a commentary of the Old Testament. Despite its inclusion of scholarship originating beyond the boundaries of traditionalism, publication of *Da'at Mikra* had been sponsored by the Rabbi Kook Institute, an Orthodox research center. Kiehl's masterpiece uses Israel's geography, botany, zoology, ecology, and secular disciplines to enhance understanding of biblical texts.

Publication of that series marks a bold move for the Orthodox institute. For many years, debate raged over whether or not to include the Pentateuch in the publication. Traditionalists feared the use of modern analytical tools to interpret what they considered to be the word of God. The decision to publish the Pentateuchal books as part of the series redounds to the institute's credit. Of course, the commentary remains within the confines of accepted Orthodox views.

I had promised the alumni group that I would take them to visit the Ebal excavation, but a torrential downpour prevented me from keeping my word. The dirt road that covers the last mile of the approach to the site had been turned into a river of mud. The group's bus would almost certainly have foundered in the mire.

The visitors had to settle for my description of our discoveries. In the course of my lecture, I noted that our findings had led us to believe that the Israelites had entered the land of Israel opposite Shechem, rather than opposite Jericho. Kiehl reminded me of a familiar biblical passage. When Joseph, the son of Jacob, was imprisoned in Egypt, he described his woes to Pharaoh's cup bearer, a fellow prisoner, who according to legend, had been thrown in jail for having allowed a fly to take a swim in Pharaoh's cup of wine. Joseph told the cup bearer that he, Joseph, had been "kidnapped from the land of the Hebrews." (Genesis 40:15.)

To what is Joseph referring? What is "the land of the Hebrews?" Why does he use the term Hebrews rather than Israelites? Earlier in Genesis, we read that when Jacob sent his son Joseph to search for his brothers, Joseph had to pass through Shechem before he found them in Dothan. The area between Shechem and Dothan parallels almost exactly the geographic territory of Mannaseh—precisely the area that we believe is the site of the Israelites' entry into Canaan. And who were the Hebrews? Abraham, the first patriarch, is described as "the Hebrew." (Genesis 14:13.) Many scholars equate the term "Hebrew" with an ancient people known as the Habiru, who are described in ancient Middle Eastern texts as marauding bands who came from the desert and as a warrior class subjugated by the local authorities. It is unclear whether the term described an ethnic or a sociological context. Abraham easily fits either type of Habiru. The Bible describes him as a nomadic shepherd with many loyal followers. He leads 318 warriors in an expedition of war against kings. When he arrives at Gerar, he considers himself a subject of its king, Abimelech.

This region, described as the land of the Hebrews, may well have been inhabited by a population sympathetic to Abraham and his followers. Perhaps Abraham's followers had themselves been the forerunners of this population. Is it not natural that the Israelite tribes, returning from Egypt to the land of their Patriarchs, would come to a region populated by their distant or not-so-distant cousins?

In that case, the Israelites wouldn't even think of destroying Shechem and its mazzeboth, and they would feel quite comfortable building their own sanctuary at Ebal, just around the corner.

Of course, it's unlikely that we will ever understand the precise nature of the relationship between the incoming Israelites and the residents of the Mannaseh territory. Nevertheless, I believe that I've had a fleeting glimpse of what lies beyond the dark, murky curtain of time.

Has my approach been rational, following a legitimate process? The answer, according to both traditional and scientific biblical scholarship, is no. Traditional interpretations do not allow us to question such biblical axioms as the Israelites' having entered Canaan opposite Jericho. And biblical science has its own axioms. The theories that have grown out of the four-source theory—J,E, P, and D — have hardened into an unbending series of "truths." I do not question the validity of the four-source concept, but I do take issue with the generally accepted dating of those materials.

Back to the settlement theories: because the evidence indicates a peaceful settlement of Mannaseh, we cannot refer to the Conquest Model to understand what transpired within the borders of Canaan during the Settlement Period. Yet, on the basis of what was going on outside of Mannaseh during this period, we must agree that the Peaceful Infiltration model also is imperfect. There is no question that at various times during the Settlement Period, Israel was conducting wars against the indigenous populations: the biblical narrative and archaeological evidence from cities that had been destroyed during this period agree on this point.

As Adam reviewed the evidence and earlier research, he began to see a picture of the Israelites' entry into Canaan that combines both models. The first step, infiltration into the Shechem area, was peaceful because there was a relationship between the "Hebrews" of Shechem and the incoming Israelites. The later stages of the settlement saw the Israelite tribes spreading throughout the land, and it was at this second stage, he posited, that the Israelite tribes waged some of the wars that are described in the books of Joshua and Judges.

And what about the third theory, the Sociological Model? How does it match up against the information gleaned from the survey of Mannaseh and the excavations at Ebal?

Despite the popularity and currency of the Sociological Model, Adam's research disproves it, point by point. This model suggests that a series of peasant revolts against Canaanite kings resulted in the formation of the tribes of Israel and their subsequent consolidation as a nation. Most of the Canaanite cities in the Late Bronze Age, which preceded the Settlement Period, were situated on the Mediterranean coast. Most of the Israelite settlements were in the central mountain region. For this model to work, we should see evidence of a population shift from the western coastal area eastward to the mountains. This, however, is not the case.

The survey gives clear indications that the earliest Settlement Period sites were located in the eastern areas, and the population progressed slowly westward. We see clear evidence of this east-to-west progress from a series of cooking pots, which Adam labeled A, B, and C. Type A pots, the oldest and most primitive, were found in the easternmost areas of Mannaseh. As we move west, we see the appearance of later, Type B pots; and finally, we see the latest, Type C pots in the westernmost areas. The archaeological findings echo the biblical texts, which trace the migration of the Israelites from east to west. On the basis of that evidence, I am confident that the Sociological Model does not hold up.

The new pottery of this era further disproves the Sociological Model. The sudden introduction of pottery of a different style during the 13th century BCE is a strong indicator that a new and different population had entered Canaan. The Sociological Model stipulates that the rebellious peasants were themselves Canaanites. If that were the case, their pottery, which dates to the Late Bronze era, should not have disappeared. To address this challenge to the Sociological Model, one of its proponents wrote an article suggesting that the disappearance of Canaanite pottery might have been due to the revolts. Possibly, the scholar wrote, all the Canaanite potters were killed during the fighting—a suggestion that implies that the potters had been singled out for destruction.

To carry this supposition to its logical conclusion, we'd have to assume that not only did the peasants do away with their potters, they also did away with all their pots, pans, and dishes. That theory is amusing at best. The introduction of a radically different kind of pottery can have been the result only of the arrival of a new population.

The Sociological Model also assumes mass conversions of the Canaanites to the Israelite religion. Although there are hints that some Canaanites merged into Israel, there is certainly no evidence that this happened on a massive scale.

To my mind, however, the most convincing challenge to that model, at least within the area of Mannaseh, is the number of Late Bronze and Settlement Period sites: there are 31 Late Bronze sites that precede the Settlement Period, and there are 140 from the Settlement Period. This signifies a considerable influx of population. Would the native peasants suddenly start multiplying like super-rabbits and build 140 towns, all the while revolting against their masters? Not likely. Just as it says in the Bible, the newer towns were built by people who came from the other side of the Jordan. And the pottery trail, moving from east to west, shows that too.

So the combined evidence of the survey and the excavations at Ebal indicate that the site was part and parcel of the entrance to the land of Israel by the people of Israel. Problem One was solved.

My second challenge was to nail down the identification of Ebal as an early Israelite cultic site.

The primary biblical source for Israelite cultic activity, as I mentioned at the beginning of this chapter, is Torat Kohanim, the Laws of the Priests, in particular

Leviticus. A familiar phrase in Leviticus reads, *He shall slaughter it at the northern side of the altar before God.* (Leviticus 1:11.) In our context, this is notable because two of Ebal's altar corners are built on an exact north-south axis. Because the Ebal structure is a seven-by-nine-meter rectangle, the other corners are not exactly on an east-west axis. There can be no question that the north-south positioning is deliberate. In the ancient Middle East, there was only one other culture that positioned cultic structures with their corners facing north, and that culture was in Mesopotamia, the birthplace of Abraham. This was the case neither in Canaan nor in Egypt.

Adam showed me that, just off the northern corner of the altar at Ebal, beyond the flat stone at its outer ledge, he had discovered signs of blood in the earth. Because the flat stone is unique among the stones of the outer ledge, it must have been put there for a purpose. We conjecture that the purpose was the slaughter of animals on the northern side of the altar, as described in Leviticus. In other words, the instructions in the priestly text perfectly describe a sacrifice that could take place at an altar situated like the one at Ebal.

On the other hand, the altar of the Second Temple, as described in the contemporaneous Mishnah, had its sides, rather than its corners, facing north and south. During the Second Temple Period, ritual animal slaughter was performed not on the altar itself, but a few meters north of the altar. So it's difficult to read our verse as a description of the setting for Second Temple sacrifices.

This comparison of the Ebal and Second Temple altars with our verse also speaks to the scholarly dating of the priestly and cultic texts, or the P source. As mentioned earlier, scholars maintain that this source, including all of Leviticus, as well as parts of Exodus and Numbers, originated rather late—probably in the Second Temple Period, after 520 BCE. But because so much of what is detailed in the P texts matches our finds at the 13th-century-BCE site in Ebal, we must consider questions about that timing. Our priestly verse from Leviticus about the northern side of the altar does not apply to the Second Temple altar, but it is right in line with our findings at a site that preceded the Second Temple by at least 700 years. This certainly indicates that some very central parts of P cannot be placed in the Second Temple Period.

Yet again, a reasonable examination of the facts indicates that Ebal can certainly be defined as an Israelite cultic site. Problem Two was solved to my satisfaction.

Before we move on to my third—and biggest—challenge, let's review some reactions of scholars to what we've discussed thus far.

In 1987, M.D. Coogan published "Of Cults and Cultures: Reflections on the Interpretation of Archaeological Evidence," in the prestigious *Palestine Exploration Quarterly*. In his article, Coogan says, "What distinguished the Israelites from their non-Israelite contemporaries was metaphysical, not physical: acceptance of Yahweh, god of Israel, and concomitant allegiance to fellow Yahwists."

Coogan admits that Ebal may be a cultic site, but he says that it likely belonged to a Canaanite—not Israelite—group. How he can make such an assumption after reading about the Ebal excavation is beyond me. In 1985, two years before Coogan's article appeared, the popular *Biblical Archaeological Review* published Adam's article about the Ebal excavation. His account describes the exact nature of the altar and the peripherals—the bone deposits and other finds—that are completely unlike any known Canaanite cultic features. On the contrary, they bear remarkable resemblance to biblical and even Mishnaic descriptions of the Second Temple altar and its associated artifacts.

Dr. Coogan's assessment makes about as much sense as saying that the celibate, robe-wearing, white-collared, bareheaded men who serve wine and wafers during Sunday morning prayer services known as masses, in buildings topped by huge crosses, might be considered Orthodox Jews.

Despite Coogan's incomprehensible statement, I must mention that he was among the very few scholars who published a reaction to Adam's publications about the Ebal excavations. Eighteen years have passed since we confirmed our identification of the central structure at Ebal as a complete burnt-offering altar, and fourteen years have elapsed since Adam's publication of his preliminary findings. Not one scientist—not even Professor Mazar—has published a single word that agrees with our conclusion. Not one word.

In June 1990 the Israel Archaeological Society held a three-day conference commemorating its 40th anniversary. The subject of cultic sites was featured on the conference agenda. Although Adam's scientific article had appeared three years earlier, he was not invited to present a lecture to this gathering. He was, however, invited to attend as a "respondent." That status would allow him to answer any questions the participants might pose to him about his work. No one asked anything.

Why? Why does Adam's remarkable research fail to earn him the attention of his colleagues and peers? Can it be that Adam's assumptions are so far removed from reality that they have made him a pariah of the scientific community?

Not at all. It is not from reality that Adam's assumptions are far removed. Rather, generally accepted scientific notions are miles away from Adam's assumptions about the process of the Settlement Period itself, the identification of such an early-stage Israelite cultic site, and problems relating to the dating of Leviticus and Deuteronomy.

Adam's survey leaves no doubt: the settlement process in Mannaseh involved both conquest and peaceful infiltration. And the identification of the site as Israelite must be disconcerting to anyone who remains mesmerized by the Sociological Model. But had the people who built the site at Ebal been disaffected Canaanites, there is no question that the site would have reflected some Canaanite cultic traditions. The site shows no Canaanite evidence and reflects exactly what is known about Israelite cultic activities, extending to the time of the Mishnah— 1,500 years after Ebal.

To accept Adam's conclusions is to toss the Sociological Model out the window. That would mean revisiting the current body of knowledge and preparing a new set of lectures. What tenured eight-hour-a-week professor wants to do that?

Now for perhaps the trickiest of all, my third challenge: Revealing the full significance of the Ebal Site.

In my opinion, the most controversial issue raised by Adam's excavations is the dating of Deuteronomy. As I noted above, the site at Ebal had been in use for as long as a century. At the end of that period—in the 12th century BCE—it was deliberately covered over and abandoned. Our excavations indicate that until Adam happened upon it some 3,300 years later, it had never before been uncovered. Is it possible that an important cultic site in northern Israel could be mentioned in the context of a book, Deuteronomy, which according to current scholarly thinking, had been written during the seventh century BCE?

Furthermore, why would any of Josiah's scribes find it necessary to include the story of the blessings and the curses in the book of Deuteronomy? The idea of this foreign material originating in the Northern Kingdom and "seeping in" is simply absurd.

The more I considered these puzzles, the more I came to believe that it was time for a new approach. Mazar had given me the confidence to ask the relevant questions, and I was developing the assuredness to present a fresh set of answers. I had to begin by answering one compound question: what was the Ebal site; what was its real significance within a historic framework; and most critical, what was its real relationship to the book of Deuteronomy?

Day and night, these questions haunted me. Then suddenly, at 3:15 a.m., on April 2, 1985, 18 months after Adam had shown me his drawing and given me the shock of my life, I awoke from a deep sleep in a cold sweat. The answer had come to me, stabbing my heart like a bolt of lightning. I was astonished. I could see that the reason the Ebal episode is in Deuteronomy is also the key to dating Deuteronomy, and in fact, most of the Pentateuch.

That morning's revelation was that Ebal was not simply the site of an altar, it was actually the site of the First Temple of Israel. Here's why:

From the time that I started my inquiries, even before Adam had deduced from the pottery that the site had been active for up to a century, I had found it hard to believe that the altar had been constructed for a single event. Building the massive structure of very large stones must have required a lot of manpower. Furthermore, the complex and difficult-to-build series of installations that enclosed large vessels as well as the double-wall enclosure bespeak a plan to use the structure with some regularity—not only once for the ceremony of the blessings and the curses.

The Talmudic sources, which I had approached first, shed little if any light on these problems. The rabbinic writings give no indication of an awareness of Ebal's installations and walls, not to mention Pharaoh's personal seal. As I became conscious of the implications of this lack, I could feel my belief in the invincibility of Orthodox doctrine beginning to crumble.

Scientific biblical scholars have also had little to say about the texts that relate to the Ebal site. I realized that I would have to rely on myself to assemble the pieces of the puzzle.

*   *   *

I started by considering the two sets of walls. For what purpose would the ancients build two sets of walls around an altar site? If it were a single wall, perhaps it could be understood as being like a Greek temenos, a wall surrounding a holy structure. But in Ebal there are two sets. Why?

I could think of only one other site that is described as having two sets of walls: the Second Temple in Jerusalem.

Among Jerusalem's most popular tourist attractions these days is a miniature model of the city as it existed during the Second Temple Period. The model, located in the Holyland Hotel in the western part of Jerusalem, was built of the local stone—just like almost every structure in Jerusalem for thousands of years. Originally built between 1964 and 1967 under the guidance of Dr. Mordechai Avi-Yonah, a professor of archaeology at the Hebrew University, the model was revised after the Six-Day War of 1967 to reflect the discoveries from excavations in territories captured during that war. I had visited this model numerous times, and when I started my research, I remembered that the model presented a construction much like the two sets of walls at Ebal.

My next thought necessitated a huge leap of faith. Could it be that the site of Ebal fulfilled a function similar to that of the Temple Mount in Jerusalem? Might it be possible that the Ebal site was itself a temple?

I turned to Maimonides, one of the greatest Jewish scholars of all time. Serving as a doctor in Egypt, late in the 13th century CE, he devoted his "spare" time to writing a considerable number of books. Among Maimonides' best-known works is his Mishne Torah, which means "repetition of the Torah." (Mishne Torah is also used as a descriptive name for the book of Deuteronomy.) Maimonides' Mishne Torah examines, point by point, all the commandments of the Pentateuch. He considers the Second Temple in a chapter called Hilchot Bet Habechira, or "Laws of the Chosen House," which, of course, is the Temple.

Which items from Maimonides' list of Second Temple attributes exist at the Ebal site? First, a burnt-offering altar: ever since Adam's workers brushed the dust of three millennia from the site, a burnt-offering altar, the centerpiece of Temple activity, has been standing proud and tall at Ebal. Next, an incense altar: we did uncover an incense altar, but, being made from stone, it does not meet the traditional criteria. As described in Exodus 30, the incense altar was gold or gold-plated. Maimonides, referring to biblical and Talmudic sources, specifically states that the incense altar should not be made of wood or stone. According to rabbinic sources, the incense altar at Ebal, which was, of course, built after the giving of the Torah at Sinai, should have conformed to the biblical description. The fact that it does not conform told me that either the biblical text was written after the events at Ebal and describes the First or the Second Temple at Jerusalem or that the biblical descriptions presented idealized renderings—not necessarily reality. Needless to say, either of these explanations leads us far beyond the boundaries of Orthodox religious doctrine.

In any case, the presence of any incense altar is a strong indicator of Temple-related activity. Coupled with the burnt-offering altar, the incense altar lends powerful support to the idea that was beginning to take shape in my mind.

I turned my attention to the two sets of walls. The walls at Ebal—even the large outer wall—were not built to provide military defense. They were no higher than one and one half meters, or five feet. By comparison, the wall that surrounds nearby Shechem is gigantic—25 feet tall, extremely thick—and offers only a few well-fortified entrances.

I was convinced that Ebal's walls had cultic symbolism and purpose. I concluded that they served the same purpose as the walls of the Temple in Jerusalem, where each one functioned as a barrier excluding a particular population. Only the priests who officiated at the altar could enter the innermost area, and their brethren, the Levites, who performed secondary tasks, were allowed access only to the larger perimeter. The walls and the entire complex at Ebal were built so that the proceedings at the altar would have been visible to anyone standing even a mile away. Such a configuration made it possible for even huge assemblies to participate in ceremonies there.

Thus, I matched three characteristics of the Temple—the burnt-offering altar, the incense altar, and the cultic barrier walls—with the findings at Ebal. The fourth characteristic was the presence of the Ark. The Bible tells us that the Israelites built the Ark in the desert to contain the tablets of the Ten Commandments. Because of its extraordinary holiness, once a year, on Yom Kippur, the Day of Atonement, the high priest alone passed through a series of curtains, entered the Holy of Holies, and stood before the Ark.

In eight seasons of excavations at Ebal, we found no indication that the Ark had ever resided there. But the presence of the Ark is mentioned in Joshua 8:33 in the description of the ceremony of the blessings and the curses. It is my guess that this description has its roots in historical reality, and that guess is supported by the consistency of the biblical story, the artifacts found at the site, and the process of the settlement. The presence of the Ark, according to the criteria set by Maimonides, would be the final indication that Ebal was indeed the site of a temple.

One afternoon after I had been struggling with my ideas for some time, I visited Adam and presented my hypotheses. He insisted then, and he still maintains, that the site should be defined as a cultic site known as a *bamah,* or biblical "high place." These high places were legitimate conduits for cultic activities during those periods when there was no central sanctuary; the Israelites were castigated for using them only when a central sanctuary was active. I believe that Adam never had the stomach to delve into a detailed study of the relations between the Ebal site and scientific biblical analysis. Being all too familiar with the kinds of controversies that rage among scholars in that field, I believe he was reluctant to tread into an area that could be even more bitter and vindictive than archaeology. Furthermore, as an archaeologist, his opinion on biblical matters would carry little weight.

It was on this point that Adam and I parted company. I looked at the evidence, and even before I began to examine the points that scientific theory defines as prerequisites for a temple, I felt in my bones that I was right. I could not imagine that a site of such intricacy and complexity, a site that had endured for so many years, could be considered anything but a temple. In an effort to give legitimacy to my gut reaction, I dedicated myself to an intensive study of all scientific materials that had any bearing on the subject of temples.

Adam loaned me a book that he himself had borrowed from Mazar. The book, *Temples and Temple Service in Ancient Israel,* was written by Professor Menahem Haran of the Hebrew University. Dr. Haran is the greatest authority on Israelite temples. He wrote the book while on a sabbatical at Oxford University, and it was published in 1978 by Oxford University Press. Haran's book is unquestionably the best source I have found for information on this subject. In addition to being a more than competent scholar, Haran is also a mensch, a good guy. He has been extremely helpful to me, spending hours of his valuable time helping me to research this subject.

In his book, Haran says that to determine whether a site has been a temple, it is critical to examine and assess four of its features, or aspects. In his own words, the four features are:

- The place (or institution)

- The time (or occasion)

- The act (or ceremony) performed

- The person (or personnel) performing it

Over the course of the past 15 years, as I sip my morning coffee, my thoughts always turn to Ebal and to Haran's four descriptive categories. Since the idea that the Ebal site might have been a temple grabbed hold of my imagination, I have remained in its powerful grip, and it will not let go.

Haran starts by considering the significance of the place or institution. The biblical mention of the Mount Ebal altar within the larger description of the apparently critical ceremony of the blessings and the curses, places it within a group of much greater importance than ordinary altars or bamah sites.

The site's elaborate design and structures reinforce the assumption of its significance. In addition to the outer and inner walls that I describe above, there is a small area enclosed by a low stone wall inside the eastern section of the outer wall. Adam guesses that it must have been a kind of corral for the sacrificial animals. A gradually inclining path with three steps that divide it into three sections leads from the 25-foot-wide entrance and connects the corral to the altar, conjuring up a mental picture of cultic processions of priests, other officiants, and the sacrificial animals. Approximately 70 round stone installations—some containing large jars, other with remnants of ash and bone—surround the altar, bearing witness to a meticulously elaborate cultic setting.

Next, Haran instructs us to consider time or occasion. The biblical text directs that the ceremony should take place *on the day you cross the Jordan* (Deuteronomy 27:2), and our findings indicate that the site was built during the earliest stages of the Settlement Period, just after the Israelites' entrance into Canaan. Several verses later, the importance of time is emphasized: *Be attentive and hear, O Israel: This day you have become a people to the Lord, your God.* (Deuteronomy 27:9.) This statement is unique in the Bible, and nowhere is there any indication that it refers to a location other than Ebal.

I am convinced that the ceremony of the blessings and the curses, which was celebrated at this Mount Ebal site upon the Israelites' entry into Canaan, marks the creation of the nation of Israel.

I was exhilarated, excited, and enchanted with the realization that, in a small way, I had helped uncover and reveal the site that my ancestors had sanctified as the birthplace of our nation. I admit that this personal revelation has had irrevocable impact on my life. Pursuing extensive textual research, I have developed a keen sensitivity that keeps me tuned to potentially relevant nuances in meaning. After so many years as a biblical-research junkie, my antennae quiver at even the slightest reference to altars, temples, and the formative years of the nation of Israel. Once when I was visiting Adam at Kibbutz Ein Shemer, he showed me a Haggadah, the liturgy for the Passover Seder. The version he showed me had been published by HaShomer Hatzair, the political movement of his kibbutz. This left-wing group could not abide the centuries-old traditional version, so it created its own, "modernizing" the texts with additions and deletions. My attention was caught by one of the new sentences, which said, in effect, that Israel became a nation at the Exodus, the celebration of which is the focus of the Passover holiday. Pointing to the sentence, I asked Adam, "After having worked for more than a decade on a project that shows that Ebal was the site of the creation of the nation of Israel, how can you, a member of this Shomer Hatzair kibbutz, sit still and allow this?"

Adam said that he had never before taken note of that verse, and he assured me that he would write to the publishers. Whether he ever did, I don't know. However, it was at that point that I realized that Ebal had colored my blood an even deeper red than Adam's.

Once we have addressed place and time, Haran directs us to consider the importance of the act or ceremony. As I have stated already, the importance of the ceremony of the blessings and the curses was such that it would not have been performed at a temporary altar. Scholars of the ancient Middle East have discovered that many cultic temples had tablets containing written affidavits that describe series of curses. In contrast to the biblical injunctions against desecrating the name of God by committing evil acts, the curses on the other cultic tablets were directed at those who would desecrate the sites or the name of the kings who had built them. Nevertheless, the motif of the curses in the biblical narrative is important in assessing the Ebal site as a temple.

Haran's fourth and final consideration is the person or personnel who officiated at the site. I feel I stand on safe ground when I assume that—like the similarly constructed walls in the Temple in Jerusalem—the outer perimeter wall and the inner temenos wall served as boundaries that defined the permissible territory for such specific populations as priests and Levites. These walls could have served no other purpose.

Thus, I am convinced that the complex discovered at Ebal corresponds to the definition of a Temple of Israel as described traditionally by Maimonides and scientifically by Haran.

When Adam and I turned to other biblical passages and stories, we saw that there were other bases for comparison and confirmation. Early in the project, when we reached the direct center of the altar, we saw a carefully built, round stone installation that was filled with a material we are still unable to identify. Adam says that the presence of this material indicates that there were two stages at Ebal: a preliminary, dedication stage, which included this installation placed directly on the bedrock, and as we discovered later, other installations surrounding it; and a second stage, which was the large stone burnt-offering altar along with the complex of walls, the entrance, and the corral.

Although the Bible describes the building of many altars, only one of those narratives suggests the necessity of building the altar in two stages. In Judges 6:19-24, the prophet Gideon offers a sacrifice on bedrock, and then, at the very same place, he builds an altar. Citing the passage, Adam provided us with a way of understanding the two-stage structure that we were looking at. Not long after that,

Mazar published an article that confirmed that the early-stage installation on the bedrock at Ebal certainly could be considered a cultic site.

Certain phrases about the ceremony of the blessings and the curses in Deuteronomy 27 are remarkably reminiscent of language that is used only to describe Temple activities: *You shall slaughter peace offerings and eat there, and you shall be glad before the Lord your God.* (Deuteronomy 27:7.) "Before the Lord," a phrase used elsewhere only in connection with the Temple, leaves the unmistakable impression that the Ebal site was a temple. The previous verse refers to burnt offerings, which like peace offerings, were mentioned exclusively in descriptions of Temple-related activities.

Nearly 3,000 bone fragments were unearthed at the Ebal site and sent to the Department of Zoology at the Hebrew University. Analysis identified the remains as the bones of cattle, sheep, goats, and fallow deer. The animals had been male yearlings, meeting the sacrificial specifications from the beginning of the book of Leviticus. Although the Bible does not include fallow deer in its lists of animals acceptable for sacrifices, at least one minority opinion in the Talmudic tractate of Pesahim states that deer could be sacrificed. It is worth noting that the deer remains were discovered exclusively in loci of Ebal's first and older phase—the dedication ceremony. I think we can reasonably assume that deer were permissible for use in the dedication ceremony, but they were forbidden at the real altar. In effect, therefore, only those animals that are described in Leviticus, were offered for sacrifice on the altar.

As details began to fill the picture, I was able to make another assumption. Such particulars as the bones, burnt-offering altar, incense altar, and outer ledge, which could be used for sprinkling the blood on the corners of the altar, indicated that the cult of Israel was fairly well developed by the time the Ebal site was built and used. In other words, the site was built in support of a well-established tradition.

Prior to Deuteronomic mentions of the altar at Ebal, the only references to organized cultic practice among the Israelites appear in the voluminous chapters of P that relate to the Tabernacle. The Tabernacle has served as another focal point for much disagreement among scholars. Did it really exist? What kind of reality, if any, does it reflect?

Wellhausen, the noted German scholar who put the source theory on the map, posited that the P material originated during the Second Temple Period and that the Tabernacle was simply a figment of the writer's imagination that reflected practices of the Second Temple. I read that to mean that biblical references to the Tabernacle were created and designed to increase the stranglehold of Second Temple priests on the wallets and pocketbooks of Israel.

Not long after Wellhausen put forth his theories, however, evidence began to emerge that indicated that portable tabernacles were part and parcel of the nomadic cultures of the ancient Middle East. Many biblical details describing Tabernacle practices don't jibe with the well-known and well-documented descriptions of Second Temple practices. Most notable is that there is no mention of the Ark during the Second Temple period. We assume that it disappeared in the destruction of the First Temple in 587 BCE. The Ark is a central feature of the P document.

Friedman, author of *Who Wrote the Bible,* puts forth an intriguing observation: the dimensions of the Ark's interior match exactly the wingspread of the cherubim, statues of winged celestial beings, that were in the Holy of Holies of Solomon's First Temple. On the basis of this evidence, we can legitimately date the P source's most important subject—the Ark—to centuries earlier than the Second Temple origins suggested by Wellhausen.

Menahem Haran has highlighted several biblical passages that, in his opinion, indicate that the Tabernacle was in reality a product of Shiloh, a central sanctuary some 20 miles south of Ebal. It existed for roughly 100 years, from about 1150 BCE until its destruction by the Philistines. So the dating of the P source in general, and the Tabernacle in particular, is slowly moving back in time. If the text in Joshua that places the Ark at the ceremony of the blessings and the curses reflects reality, then the Ark existed even before Shiloh.

Now let's assemble all this information and view it from a sequential, historical perspective. The third challenge was revealing the full significance of the Ebal site. I now had clear evidence that the the biblical texts had originated at the time the site was active, and I was subsequently able to redefine Ebal as a temple.

Because the findings at Ebal indicate a well-developed set of cultic practices, Ebal as a cultic site must have been preceded by earlier stages. We may assume there were earlier stages because the biblical narrative describes the nomadic wanderings of the Israelites. (Some scholars, particularly those who support the Sociological Model, disagree with that.) If we consider this in light of archaeological evidence that during that period, other Middle Eastern cultures had portable shrines similar to the biblical Tabernacle, we find that that the biblical descriptions of the Tabernacle do contain more than a grain of truth. Once I had reached that conclusion, it was reasonable to assume that the installation at Ebal replaced the Tabernacle. At Ebal, I believe, the Israelites established their permanent presence, building their first sanctuary—the First Temple of Israel—in the land.

To help me keep all my ideas straight, I tried to define the sequence of Israelite sanctuaries: first a portable desert Tabernacle, then Ebal, then Shiloh, then a number of lesser sites that temporarily housed the Ark following its capture by and recapture from the Philistines, and then finally the Temple in Jerusalem.

The Mishnah, in chapter 14 of the tractate of Zebahim, recognizes this sequence, with the exception of Ebal, in its determination of the point in Israelite history when it was no longer permissible to sacrifice outside a central sanctuary. Of course, because the compilers of the Mishnah had no inkling of what went on at Ebal, Ebal does not appear in its list of sanctuaries. Roland De Veaux, a Catholic priest and brilliant biblical scholar, compiled his own list, which is similar to that of the Mishnah. De Veaux worked at archaeology in Israel for many years, but he, too, missed the importance of Ebal.

Up to that point in my research, I had little to support my belief that the Ebal site had been a temple: only congruencies of the site with the known functions of the Second Temple. The details as set forth by both Maimonides and Haran reflected extensive descriptions from the Talmud, as well as such independent outside sources as Josephus Flavius, the Jewish general-turned-Roman-historian, who himself was a priest and had actually served in the Temple. I believed that the sequence of sanctuaries I had defined would also support my theory. Still, I asked myself, Why is there no statement within the biblical narrative itself that indicates that Ebal had been a temple? Before I could assert with any certainty that Ebal had been a temple, indeed the First Temple of Israel, I had to identify supporting evidence in the Bible. If the writer or writers of the passages relating to Ebal had influenced the shaping of the Bible—as obviously they had—I was sure that there would be some trace of the Ebal story elsewhere in the text.

But search as I did, after the passages in the book of Joshua, I could find not a single biblical reference to Ebal. The reason for this came to me in the middle of one night in August 1985. When I was awakened by this sudden realization, I had to wonder not only why it had never before occurred to me, but also why no one else had thought of it.

As fate would have it, the following day I would be meeting Professor Mazar in Haifa at the university's archaeological museum. The two of us had been engaged in a decade-long conversation about whether or not the site at Ebal was a temple. And the professor's conclusion always was, *Ya, ya, nisht, nisht,* which in Yiddish means, "maybe yes, maybe no." Some of Adam's findings had been placed on display at the museum, and a number of scholars, including Mazar, had been invited for the festive occasion. Waiting very impatiently until after all the presentations, I virtually ran over to Mazar, and told him my previous night's revelation. Over the years, I had spent dozens of hours discussing almost everything under the sun with him, but for the very first time since we first met, he was really impressed. With evident excitement, he grabbed my hand and said, "This you must write down." It was that fervent command that led me to write this book.

I had told him that I was convinced that the answer to our decade-long debate could be found in Genesis 48 and that if my interpretation of that chapter is correct, the events described there never took place.

Joseph, whom his brothers had sold into slavery, had become second-in-command to Pharaoh in Egypt. Because his brothers were suffering famine in his native land, Canaan, Joseph invited them along with their father, Jacob, to come to Egypt, where they would share in Joseph's good fortune. They accepted his invitation. Some time later, when Jacob was near death, he blessed his children as well as his grandsons, Mannaseh and Ephraim, Joseph's sons.

The biblical narrative tells us that Joseph brought his two sons to his father for the patriarchal blessing. Joseph was careful to place Mannaseh, his first born, at his own left, and Ephraim, the younger, at his right, so that when the three of them—Manneseh, Joseph, and Ephraim—were facing Jacob, he would place his right hand, the more important, atop the head of the first born, Mannaseh, and his left hand atop the head of Ephraim, the younger son.

Jacob, however, pulls a switch. He crosses his arms, one over the other, placing his right hand atop Ephraim's head and his left atop Mannaseh's. A bemused Joseph attempts to reposition his father's hands, but Jacob resists. When Joseph asks Jacob to explain this strange behavior, Jacob says, I know, my son, I know. He [Mannaseh] too will become a people, and he too will become great; yet his younger brother [Ephraim] shall become greater than he, and his seed will fill many nations. (Genesis 48:19.)

There can be no question that the purpose of this chapter was to present an explanation for Ephraim's predominance over Mannaseh. When did this predominance occur? When was it relevant? And last, but certainly not least, how did this predominance manifest itself?

Why *did* Jacob cross his arms?

The answer should have been obvious to me for the four years preceding that early morning in August. The day before, I had been reading about Shiloh. Finkelstein, who had conducted the most recent excavation of Shiloh, had dated the origins of the city as an Israelite cultic site to 1150 BCE of the Iron Age. Adam had dated Ebal's origins to sometime in the period stretching from 1250 through 1220 BCE. He was certain that the site had ceased to exist by 1150 BCE, a date that coincides exactly with Shiloh's early days as a cultic center. Ebal is located in the biblical area that was allotted to Manasseh. Shiloh was in the area allotted to Ephraim.

I now understand that the passage in Genesis 48 is there to provide an explanation for the transfer of the Israelites' central holy site from Ebal, which belonged to Mannaseh, to Shiloh, which was in the region that belonged to Ephraim.

Biblical commentators have explained that Jacob crossed his arms so that the younger son would get his blessing. Rashi, the most prolific and highly respected of the traditional Jewish commentators, writes that the incident describes the relative merits of the future descendants of Mannaseh and Ephraim. Gideon, a descendant of Mannaseh, was an important figure in Israel, but Joshua, the descendant of Ephraim, was more important. Being able to see the future, Jacob placed his right hand on the head of the younger son, Ephraim, whose descendents would be more important than those of his brother, Mannaseh.

Others have noted that throughout the biblical narrative it is almost inevitable that the younger son will achieve greater prominence than his elder: Abel, the younger son of Adam, was recognized as the better son and was slain by his older brother, Cain; although the Koran would have you believe otherwise, Isaac, Abraham's younger son, continues the patriarchal line rather than Ishmael; and Jacob, in place of his older twin brother, Esau, becomes the third patriarch.

I maintain that neither of these explanations is adequate to explain the very elaborately emphatic narrative presented in Genesis 48. The background for this chapter has to have been an event of national significance and moment.

And that event must have been the relocation of the central holy site of Israel.

I found supporting evidence for my interpretation in the next chapter. Jacob gives blessings to each of his sons, and in his blessing of Judah, Jacob says, "The scepter shall not depart from Judah, nor the lawmaker from between his legs, until Shiloh arrives and nations will gather to him." (Genesis 49:10.) Rashi, who can make no connection between Shiloh, the sanctuary, and Judah, interprets Shiloh as the Messiah.

But I disagree. Shiloh has only one meaning in the Bible. It is the physical site that served as the central sanctuary. Although the exact meaning of that verse is unclear, it does place Shiloh within the context of Jacob's blessings, not only as a general reference, but also as a place of hope for the future. Clearly, the author of Genesis 48 and 49 recognizes Shiloh's importance. And its importance in the Bible was associated only with its being the location of the sanctuary.

Searching for biblical references to Shiloh, I came across a fascinating detail in the book of Jeremiah. As a conduit for the words of God, Jeremiah, the "Prophet of Doom," tells of the Babylonians' destruction of the First Temple: *So go to My place that is in Shiloh, where I placed My name for the first time, and see what I did to it because of the evil of My people, Israel.* (Jeremiah 7:12.)

The phrase, *the Place that He will choose,* appears 34 times in Deuteronomy to describe the Temple. The mention in Jeremiah is the first and only specific biblical indication that that "the Place" does not necessarily refer to Jerusalem. Jeremiah is said to have descended from a family of priests that served at Shiloh. And according to the Mishnah, outside of Jerusalem, Shiloh was the only site in Israel that was a full-blown central sanctuary. One factor differentiated Jerusalem and Shiloh from all other holy sites in Israel: in both these places, Centralization of the Cult was in effect, and it was forbidden to conduct sacrifices elsewhere.

That Centralization of the Cult was in effect at Shiloh is borne out by a story in Joshua 22. Two and a half tribes of Israel had settled on the east bank of the Jordan before the rest of the Israelites had entered the land. The early arrivals had built an altar near the Jordan, raising an uproar among the rest of the tribes, who congregated at Shiloh to prepare to attack their brethren. A group of Israel's leaders, headed by Phineas, a great-nephew of Moses, set out to chastise the errant tribes. The nature of their crime is clear: they had built an altar at a time that the central sanctuary at Shiloh existed.

In their defense, the two and a half tribes said that they had built the altar not for sacrifices, but only as a monument that would remind them of their affiliation with the other tribes of Israel. Phineas accepted their explanation, and peace reigned. This story establishes Centralization long before Jerusalem and King David.

My thinking was that if Shiloh had replaced Ebal, the same rules that the Mishnah applied to Shiloh and Jerusalem would also be relevant to Ebal. And, I thought, if my assumption is correct, then Ebal—not Shiloh, and not even Jerusalem—is the place that Deuteronomy calls *the Place that He will choose.*

On the face of it, my idea seemed absurd. Traditional and scientific sources agreed on at least one point: Jerusalem was "the Place." Traditional religious interpreters view it as part of the Mosaic prophesy, and scientific scholars understand it to be part and parcel of Josiah's attempt to centralize the cult in his own capital, Jerusalem. Nevertheless, I sat down with a Bible and a stack of other volumes and started looking for evidence that would support my assumption.

The first thing I noticed is that identification of "the Place" as Jerusalem is actually problematic. Although Jerusalem is mentioned 688 times in the Hebrew Bible, it is never mentioned in the book of Deuteronomy, where *the Place that He will choose* appears 34 times. Only one sacred site is mentioned in Deuteronomy— a book dedicated to the proposition of Centralization of the Cult — Ebal.

In order to identify Ebal as "the Place," I knew that I needed to find evidence that would link Ebal to texts related to "the Place." Explicit references linking the two do not exist. However, there are implicit suggestions that point in this direction. Many scholars have made reference to the activities at Ebal described in Deuteronomy 27, noting that the verses seemed to be describing Temple activity. But they have simply shrugged their shoulders and dismissed the curious coincidence, pointing out that as the book is in the D source it had been compiled during the time of Josiah and could not be describing Temple activity in Ebal.

Time was the first link that came to my mind. If Ebal is indeed "the Place," there must be evidence that links the site and its biblical description to a particular time that has no relevance to Jerusalem. That time would have to have been during the Settlement Period, before Jerusalem became the eternal center of Israel. But very few biblical texts antedate tenth century BCE. Is there evidence that the Ebal story fits into this category? As mentioned earlier, Deuteronomy 27 and Joshua 8 describe the altar as being "in" Mount Ebal. (This distinction, between "in" and "on," is found only in what is known as the MT, or Masoretic Text, the traditional Hebrew text. Certainly no English versions, based on Greek and Latin translations, pick this up.) If, as I have noted earlier, the altar was deliberately covered, how could Josiah's scribes, 600 years later, have known that it was "in" Mount Ebal?

I've presented my ideas to a number of scholars, including Haran, and each of them has rejected the legitimacy of my argument. Haran maintains that the use of "in" rather than "on" may very well be arbitrary. I disagree. That might have been the case had there been only one use of "in" versus "on." The three comparisons and distinctions are, in my opinion, too much for coincidence.

Simple, straightforward reasoning tells us that the Ebal text is very old, written by people who saw or heard firsthand accounts about the site, knew that it was "in" Mount Ebal, and described it in Temple-like terms because it actually was known to them as a temple. The essential Deuteronomic story must have originated at about the time that Ebal was active.

Deuteronomy contains two separate mentions of the ceremony of the blessings and the curses: Deuteronomy 11:26-30 and the longer description in Deuteronomy 27. What lies between those two occurrences?

A passage known as the Law Code of Deuteronomy (Deuteronomy 12-26) intervenes between the first and second mentions of the ceremony of the blessings and the curses. The Code presents laws related to "the Place." In fact, 19 of Deuteronomy's 34 mentions of "the Place" can be found in those chapters.

I imagined myself as source D, the nameless scribe responsible for compiling and editing Deuteronomy. To introduce a Law Code about a temple, a brief mention or an introduction about its location would be in order. And indeed, the Law Code is preceded by the introduction to the ceremony of the blessings and the curses that marked the building of the temple at Ebal (Deuteronomy 11:26-30). As the scribe, I would follow the introductory material with a summation of the laws relating to that temple, and conclude with a summary of the ceremony at the dedication of the temple.

And that is precisely the structure of the biblical narrative. If the Ebal material serves as both a preface and an appendix to the Law Code, it must have been placed there willfully—not whimsically. I consider this strong textual evidence for relating Ebal to the core of what is known as Centralization of the Cult.

Strangely enough, my far-ranging research led me to the English philosopher Thomas Hobbes. In his *Leviathan,* Hobbes gave me a reasonable explanation for the sequence of events surrounding Centralization. Hobbes reviews the story of Josiah and the discovery of the scroll by his high priest, Hilkiya. Finding the story credible, Hobbes defines the contents of that scroll as the Law Code of Deuteronomy, which emphasized Centralization. The concept of Centralization, he suggests, although it had existed for many years, had been lost and subsequently rediscovered during the time of Josiah.

When and how did the Deuteronomic Law Code and—probably with it—the Ebal references disappear? My guess is that this happened during the tumultuous period that followed the Philistines' capture of the Ark at Shiloh, around 1050 BCE. If that assumption is correct, the Law Code would have existed for 100 to 200 years, through the periods of Ebal and Shiloh. I have shown evidence that during the period of Shiloh, Centralization was a factor, and even the Mishnah retains memory of this. But apparently the concept of Centralization was lost for the greater part of the First Jerusalem Temple period, when there is no evidence that Centralization was required and there are many mentions of sacrifices at various other places.

In I Kings 18, we see an extraordinary biblical dramatization of this. The prophet Elijah challenges and is victorious over the false prophets of the Canaanite god Ba'al by presenting a miraculously self-igniting sacrifice at Mount Carmel. It is difficult to imagine how the Bible could present the story of Elijah's sacrifice had the concept of Centralization been known and accepted during that era, roughly 850 BCE, 100 years after the Temple in Jerusalem had been built.

The ramifications of my assumption for biblical dating are revolutionary, to say the least. The dating of Deuteronomy has long been the foundation from which the dates of the other biblical sources were derived. If the theories I have put forth are correct, that foundation is open to serious question. Identification of "the Place" as Ebal means that Deuteronomy contains the oldest-known biblical material. Although it is regarded as the fifth Book of Moses, it may very well have been the first one written.

Does a few hundred years in the dating of these texts make any real difference? It certainly does. Consider this example. When the Amish settled in Pennsylvania about 300 years ago, they named one of their towns Intercourse, a name nobody would give to a U.S. town these days. In the 300 years that have passed since the founding of Intercourse, Pennsylvania, there have been changes in how people hear that word and the associations it conjures up in our minds. Language changes. Any interpretation of texts that is based on faulty dating, therefore, may be flawed and possibly even nonsensical. And since scientific biblical dating is founded on the concept of source D being a product of the seventh century BCE, in my opinion, almost all of today's scientific biblical research rests on faulty dating.

Let me point out one other implication of my assumption that Ebal is "the Place." If "the Place" chosen by God is not Jerusalem, Jerusalem's theological relevance is questionable.

And this has ramifications not only for Jewish theology. The interest of Christians and Moslems in Jerusalem is based upon the Jews' identification of Jerusalem as "the Place." What I am saying is that the three religions that are rooted in monotheism have not preserved the original intent of a most vital theme in the Hebrew Bible: the memory of the real *Place that He will choose to put His name* there. The implications are far-reaching.

If my assumptions are correct, the age-old longing for Jerusalem has been misguided. If Jerusalem is not "the Place," then the Crusades, which were initiated for the purpose of capturing the city from Moslem infidels, were a monumental waste of lives, time, energy, and money. Likewise, lacking a religious connection to the city, the Arabs' struggle for hegemony in Jerusalem has no theological meaning.

But unlike Christianity and Islam, the Jewish connection to Jerusalem is not a purely religious connection. For Jews, the connection to Jerusalem has also been historical. Jerusalem has been the only real capital of Israel, and Jerusalem has been a real capital only for Israel. It was from Jerusalem that the House of David ruled for four centuries; it was to Jerusalem that the exiled Jews returned to build the Second Temple around 517 BCE; and it was to Jerusalem that Jews returned en masse two thousand years later.

*   *   *

I have taken you on a tour that has revisited the entrance of the Israelites into their land during the Settlement Period, the sequence of Israelite cultic sites, and evidence that indicates that Ebal was a temple. The culmination of that trip is, of course, the most significant point of interest: Ebal was the Temple, "the Place," the Lost Temple of Israel.

Why has this story received almost no publicity or recognition? The results of the excavations at Ebal have raised astonishing questions with potentially staggering answers. Why have you read nothing about it in the *New York Times*? Why has *60 Minutes* never reported our results? Why have the excavations at Ebal never been a topic of discussion at a scholarly convention? In Numbers, the next chapter, I present the answers—my answers—to these questions, as well as a description of the current situation at Ebal, which the Intifada has put almost beyond our reach. Almost, but not quite.

Numbers

And we have brought the Lord's offering, what each
man found, vessels of gold, anklet and bracelet,
ring, earring, and clasp, to atone for our souls
before the Lord. (Numbers 31:50.)

The book of Numbers tells us that following a successful battle against the Midianites, the Israelite military commanders made an offering at the desert temple, or Tabernacle, of the booty they had taken from the Midianites. Whether or not the commanders did indeed make an offering in gratitude to God, I can't say. It's quite possible that the passage was inserted by the P source in an effort to encourage such offerings. I can say, however, that certain of the items that are mentioned in that passage—the earrings, bracelet, and rings—figure in the Ebal story. In one of the installations, we found gold and silver earrings of Egyptian design, as well as a bronze ring and bracelets, apparently a gift presented to God at the sanctuary at Ebal.

If we had been in a position to sell those gold and silver earrings, certified as authentic gifts that had been presented to God at the First Israelite Temple at Ebal, I imagine they would have fetched a tidy sum at Sotheby's. No longer would Adam's archaeological projects need to go begging. Unfortunately, a sale was not an option. Archaeologists must report every valuable item they unearth to Israel's Department of Antiquities. The discoveries are considered property of the Israeli government. Over the years, there have been numerous proposals urging the liberalization of laws related to the antiquities. Why shouldn't the government sell items that are not museum quality and use the proceeds to support archaeological research?

Such problems pale in the face of harsh reality, and I consider myself fortunate simply to have survived long enough to have had opportunities to deal with such issues. On August 1, 1983, at 11:36 p.m., I was shot at and wounded by Arab terrorists. That day was the anniversary of my father-in-law's death, and our family's annual custom was to visit his gravesite in Natanya. Our two older boys, Eyal and Aviad, who at the time were 11and 9, had gone on a camping trip, and four-year old Ori was spending the night with friends. So my wife Ofra and I were in no particular rush to return home. We decided to see a movie before returning to Shavei Shomron.

The film ended a few minutes after 11:00 p.m. Natanya is on the Mediterranean coast, a 35-minute drive east to the hills of Samaria. Ten minutes into the trip, we arrived at the train tracks that mark Israel's pre-1967 border with Jordan. This imaginary Green Line separates Israel from the West Bank. Due east of Natanya, we were at the narrowest part of the country.

I drove over the train tracks and made a left to get to the Tulkarm-Shechem road. Tulkarm is the first of the Arab towns that we'd pass as we drove to Shavei Shomron, and we skirted around it from the north. Because of the late hour, there was nothing to see but stray cats and dogs and the occasional mule. Moslem law forbids the drinking of alcohol, and the very thought of a discotheque like those in Natanya is sacrilegious. Consequently, the West Bank offers little in the way of nightlife.

Back in 1983, Israeli army patrols were scarce, and we saw none as we made our way home. Just beyond Tulkarm, we passed Nur-Champs, a Palestinian refugee camp known for harboring extremists. Five years later, the Israeli army responded to intifada violence and rooftop stone-throwing by building a gigantic fence along the road that borders Nur-Champs and deploying an entire platoon of soldiers to the first hill east of the camp.

At the next junction, a road leads to Bal'a, a small town situated on a nearby hill. As we drove by, I couldn't help thinking about an event that had taken place one Sunday morning a few months earlier. As our school's cook was riding to work from Natanya, hidden terrorists shot at the bus as it passed through this junction. Unfortunately for the gunmen, the bus was filled with paratroopers returning to the Jordan Valley after the weekend. It took the soldiers only minutes to shoot and kill the two terrorists.

Anabta is the only town on our route through which the road actually passes. A fairly large town of more than 3,000 residents at the time, it has always provided a lot of work for Israel's security apparatus. A good number of terrorist cells associated with PLO factions in Damascus had formed in Anabta.

As we drove out of the town, I unconsciously breathed a sigh of relief. But that relief was short-lived. From the corner of my eye, I saw a brilliant flash of light bursting about three yards away. As I realized that I had seen the flash of a rifle, the sound of shots rang out, and one of the shells pierced the passenger door. Neither of us was hit directly, but the bullet lodged into the door next to me, and shrapnel from the door of the car pierced our legs.

Acting instinctively, I grabbed the microphone of our emergency-communications radio and called the military command at Shechem. Initially, the soldiers greeted my report as if it were a hoax. But it didn't take long for me to convince them that the attack was real.

As I spoke with the soldiers, I was checking our bloodied legs. I was relieved to see that no major arteries had been severed. Realizing that I wasn't in such bad shape, I thought that maybe I should stop the car and shoot it out with the terrorists. At that point in the road, however, streetlights bathe the area in bright light: we would be very visible targets to the terrorists cloaked in darkness. Furthermore, reason reminded me that the range of my Beretta .22 handgun was no match for their rifles.

My call to the military base had been monitored by the two members of my town who were on guard duty that night, and using their transmitters, they instructed me to continue driving another ten minutes until I reached the Deir Sharaf junction, only 800 meters from the town. Our town's ambulance and nurse would be there to meet us.

The nurse, Leah, one of the most competent medical people I have ever known, examined our legs, cleaned them, applied temporary bandages, and told us that we should certainly go to a hospital for urgent treatment. As Leah was conducting her preliminary examination and bandaging our wounds, a military jeep arrived, and the army personnel started to question me about every detail of the shooting incident.

When our ambulance set out for the hospital, the army jeep came too, and ten minutes later, we were again passing through Anabta, going in the opposite direction. Green-beret border police were already conducting the search for terrorists.

Haim, the ambulance driver, had a long history as a paramedic, and he felt it was his duty to lighten the emotionally charged atmosphere. So he kept us amused by telling an endless string of gory horror tales. I have to admit that Ofra was the more stoic of the two of us. As the ambulance covered the darkened route to the hospital, her chief concern was what we would tell our children.

That certainly was not the first time I had been shot at, but it was the first time I had been wounded. I had been shot at when I was in combat, but those times I had been prepared for and expecting enemy fire. For some reason, I found that being the victim of terrorists was a humiliating experience. I was shocked that an unseen enemy could so violently and brutally violate my privacy. At first, I was consumed by the most primitive thoughts of revenge. But I knew that what I wanted was to vent my anger. Had I ever really wanted to seek vengeance for the Arabs' attacks on settlers like me and my family, I had had plenty of opportunities. I would never resort to cowardly acts like theirs.

It was about 1:00 a.m. when we arrived at the emergency room of the hospital in Kfar Saba. A young doctor examined our bloodied legs, and determining that our wounds were not serious, he proceeded to remove every piece of shrapnel he could find. He encountered few problems as he operated on my wife's legs, but in my legs, he identified two pieces of shrapnel that were too deep to reach without extensive cutting. He told me, however, that at some point in the future, my body would probably reject those pieces: they would simply rise to the surface and disappear sometime when I was showering or bathing.

I'm sorry to say that his optimism was unwarranted. Two of the pieces had lodged in a nerve beneath my right knee, and subsequent consultation with one of Israel's leading orthopedic surgeons confirmed that because the shrapnel was embedded in a vital nerve, surgery was not an option. I didn't then, nor do I now, feel at all sanguine about the likelihood of amputation, so I have been enduring the pain. I admit, however, that I am able to provide extremely accurate forecasts of changes in barometric pressure, at least 24 hours in advance.

Within a half-hour of our arrival at the hospital, we were already making our way back to Shavei Shomron. When we reached Anabta an hour or so later, we found the eastern outskirts of the town as busy as Grand Central Station in New York City. Dozens of vehicles from the army, border police, and Shin Bet (Israel's counterintelligence and internal security service) lined the road. Our first reaction was that they were searching for evidence related to the shooting.

But when I saw that the search was focused at least one kilometer east of where we had been ambushed, I shouted at Haim that he should stop the ambulance. I stumbled out and hobbled over to identify myself to the military guards. Once I had assured myself of a ride home, I told Haim he should leave me and take Ofra back to Shavei Shomron.

I had described the exact location of the attack both when I had radioed the army post during the shooting itself and then again when we met the soldiers at the Deir Sharaf junction. I couldn't understand why they would be searching so far from the right place.

I questioned the officer in charge, the chief inspector who was the Border Police commander of Judea and Samaria. He told me that 15 minutes after we were shot at, a bus carrying only equipment and a single paratroop sergeant had followed our route. Although shots had been fired at the bus as well, none of them had found their mark. The investigators had interrogated the sergeant about the incident, but he had incorrectly identified the source of the shots. Insisting that the chief inspector let me show him the precise location, I sat myself in the front passenger seat of his jeep and directed him toward the town. Turning east, we retraced the route I had driven earlier that night.

After driving some 100 yards, I asked him to stop. We got out of the car and there, not even four feet from where I stood, we found the five empty rifle cartridges that had been the object of his three-hour search.

It was shocking to realize that even though the border police had arrived in Anabta from Tulkarm only seven minutes after my having reported the incident, the terrorists had remained in their ambush and were comfortably positioned to shoot at the bus 15 minutes later. Had the army given the border police the exact location as I had described it and when I had described it, they would have been able to catch the bastards red-handed.

To say that I was annoyed is an understatement. But I have to say that I was not at all prepared to learn that the army's neglect was matched by comparable neglect by Shin Bet.

Within a week of the attack, an Arab friend from a neighboring town paid us a call and during the course of his visit, he told us that watermelon rinds had been found near the empty cartridges. Apparently the terrorists had been biding their time, enjoying the summer night in the normal Middle Eastern fashion. My friend told me that he had been at a Nablus café, where he'd overheard conversations about the shooting. It seems that the terrorists who had shot the Yahud, "Jew" in Arabic, had purchased their watermelon from a dealer who lived in Ramin, a town near the site of the shooting.

Believing that this information would be critically important to the investigators of the incident, that very afternoon I drove to the Tulkarm Shin Bet office, which had jurisdiction over Anabta. To my great surprise and astonishment, the operative to whom I spoke had no interest in hearing the story. With unparalleled arrogance, he announced, "I deal only with Arabs, not with Jews!"

It was nearly two years later that I had an early-morning phone call from a friend in Shin Bet. He told me that the perpetrators had been apprehended. They belonged to a PLO terrorist group known as the Democratic Front for the Liberation of Palestine (DFLP), which was led by Naif Hawatma. In the time since my shooting, DFLP had continued its terrorist activities, and at their trial, the terrorists were found guilty of murdering an Arab taxi driver, whom they suspected of cooperating with Shin Bet. As a matter of fact, they were wrong about that, and it galls me that official negligence may have cost that poor soul his life.

The night of the shooting, I arrived home at 4:15 a.m., and less than three hours later, I received my first visitor, Benny Katzover, head of the Shomron Regional Council and one of the leaders of Gush Emunim. We were on friendly terms, so his visit was more than official inquiry about the ambush. I had only one request. I wanted to keep the story out of the public spotlight. I reasoned that it would be counterproductive to publicize the event. After all, publicity could only detract from our efforts to attract new residents to the settlements. He agreed and deflected the media's requests for interviews that day.

Despite his silence, the report the police had filed after interviewing us at the Kfar Saba hospital had come to the attention of the media. We had made successful efforts to keep our names out of the news because we wanted to avoid the inevitable flood of phone calls from friends and relatives. But radio reports mentioned our town, Shavei Shomron, and we and everyone else who lived in Shavei Shomron were overwhelmed with phone calls from worried family and friends.

A continuous flow of neighbors filed through our tiny apartment, and we insisted that everyone agree not to speak to the press. As chairman of our town council, I met the various press crews that visited the town for story details. I told them that the car had been taken to the police for ballistics tests (I myself had taken it there earlier that day), and it was therefore inaccessible. I also asserted that because the unnamed, wounded couple had left town to get some peace and quiet, there was really no story, and they might as well leave. I delivered my stock speech dressed in my standard summer garb—a T-shirt, shorts, and sandals. That day, however, my leg was wrapped in an enormous bandage that reached from my ankle to my thigh. I was amazed and gratified that nobody remarked on or connected the bandage with the shooting. I suspected that one newsman from ABC-TV was suspicious, but my presentation was so emphatic that he gave up and left with his crew, cameras, and other paraphernalia.

If ever I needed confirmation that by and large newspaper stories are far from accurate, I don't anymore. Seven Israeli newspapers picked up the story, and each of them reported different and contradictory details about the incident. Only one newspaper reported it with any degree of accuracy. Because I know that its account was extracted from Shin Bet reports to which it should have no access, I will not name that paper. The correspondent at that newspaper was an erstwhile employee of Shin Bet. For obvious reasons, his earlier association with the security agency was far from public.

A few days after the shooting, I phoned Adam, who, having missed the reports in the newspapers, was completely surprised. Nivi called me to see how I was getting on. I visited them a few days later and could read the relief in their faces when they saw for themselves that I had survived the attack with a minimum of damage.

Whenever I think back to that night, I am reminded of life's unpredictability. Like a dry twig, life can be snapped short in an instant. Knowing firsthand just how fragile our lives can be, I was more determined than ever to find a solution to the puzzle of Ebal. I am pleased to say that my attempts to find this solution were much more exhilarating than the shooting incident. In this intellectual struggle, I had to overcome not Arab terrorists but an enormous mountain of books and well-entrenched theories that had formed and grown over generations. Never satisfied only to read the opinions of the experts, I made a point of meeting with them: rabbinical scholars, university professors, museum curators, and any others who might help me unravel these mysteries.

The first season of the excavations, in April 1982, had been conducted with fewer than ten people, all of whom were Adam's friends and acquaintances. I had been able to persuade my town council to allow the group free use of a few field-school rooms, so the question of finances had not posed a great problem.

However, as a result of the first season's results, the needs would be more difficult to meet. The preparatory work of the first season had focused on mapping the site and clearing away stones and other obstacles from the rarely used dirt road that approaches the site.

It had become obvious, however, that to be productive in the following seasons of the excavations, we would need dozens of volunteers, trained archaeologists to supervise, specialized equipment, as well as the skills and expertise of photographers and artists. Together, Adam and I devoted countless hours to trying to get a handle on our precise needs for subsequent seasons of excavations.

Adam concluded that to achieve more than simply a literal scratching of the surface, he would need 30 to 40 volunteers a week for three or more weeks every season. Of course, those volunteers would have to be housed, fed, and transported to the site, a 45-minute drive from Shavei Shomron.

Had Adam been a famous archaeologist like Yadin, and had the dig been situated in Jerusalem, we would have had fewer problems. However, being out in the sticks, especially in the West Bank, meant that we encountered enormous obstacles when we tried to enlist volunteer help. I turned first to the Ministry of Education, which had provided much of the financing for our field-school operation. I was able to arrange for subsidies that would support groups of high school students' participation. But even with that approval, I was faced with the challenge of finding groups willing to undertake the week of demanding work. Every day would begin at 3:30 a.m. Then, after eight to nine hours of manual labor at the site, the workers would need to spend two additional hours washing pottery back at our camp at Shavei Shomron.

It wasn't easy, but with the help and connections of the field school staff, we did manage to recruit a few groups of students, who, it turns out were exclusively from religious high schools. The students were eager and our description of what they would be doing kindled their genuine enthusiasm for the difficult work. At the same time, Adam had recruited a group of female students from a kibbutz-based teacher's seminary, and I found it amusing to watch the Orthodox high-school boys working alongside the casually—and scantily—dressed girls.

Benny Katzover's Shomron Regional Council provided some financing. But Adam was somewhat uncomfortable about that support. Every municipality and regional council in Israel makes a practice of supporting scientific endeavors that take place within their regions. But our situation was unique. The council, dominated by Gush Emunim, was supporting a dig that was being directed by an archaeologist from a Hashomer Hatzair kibbutz. Gush Emunim and Hashomer Hatzair are at opposite ends of Israel's political spectrum. Adam worried that by accepting that funding, he was making himself vulnerable to accusations of having "sold out." Gush Emunim propaganda had always stressed that the West Bank territories must never return to Arab rule because the Bible specifies that those areas are part of the Land of Israel. Adam's research and especially the excavations at Ebal reinforced that claim. Adam and I had discussed this problem endlessly, and we did everything in our power to keep his scientific undertakings from being politicized.

For nearly two years we succeeded. But in October 1983, soon after the eventful third season during which we became aware of the similarities of the altar at Ebal and the Mishnaic descriptions of Israelite altars, Adam finally felt the confidence to present his findings. It didn't take long for the proverbial manure to hit the fan.

Adam had told his colleagues and administrators at Haifa University, where he taught, about the astonishing finds of the third season. The university's public relations department, which had decided to release the news to the press, scheduled a trip to the site within weeks of the season's close. Rather than being a great step forward, the press trip turned out to be a monumental headache, and we found ourselves in the a midst of a political stew.

Adam asked me to do him the favor of meeting a group of journalists at the Deir Sharaf junction—where the ambulance had collected my wife and me after the shooting three months earlier—and accompanying them from there to the site.

It would have been far more convenient to ask them to wait at Shavei Shomron, just up the road, but Adam wanted to do whatever he could to keep the journalists thinking about the dig itself rather than focusing on his ties to both Shavei Shomron and Gush Emunim. Adam took precautions, but he couldn't control what happened.

Adam's presentation to the press was clothed in the kind of hesitation all scientists use to state their claims. He hedged every sentence, qualifying every statement with a maybe, possibly, perhaps, it-might-be-reasonable-to-assume-that, and the like. "Maybe this is an Israelite altar." "Possibly, this slanted row of stones is a ramp." "Perhaps this structure is the one referred to in the Bible." Although I was well acquainted with the scholarly application of such terminology, I found those endless qualifications about our findings at Ebal completely maddening. I knew that like me, Adam felt strongly that the discovery could be described in definitive terms. But in the academic world, absolute declarations are anathemas. Only if his presentation had included a video of Joshua describing the site and claiming it as his own would Adam have felt that he was in a position to define his results in more aggressive terms.

Despite Adam's restraint, his description should have been enough to make headlines around the world. Even at that early stage of investigation, the strong possibility that the site could be associated with specific verses of the Bible should have made Adam's presentation newsworthy.

The results of the news conference were sorely disappointing. Most of the reporters devoted considerable ink to a discussion of contemporary Israeli politics and how the political situation was at work in Ebal. The reporters seem to have had a field day—but not about the findings in the field. One article, by the Associated Press, was particularly vicious. The American reporter who wrote the item had spent the previous three years in Egypt. No doubt that was where she had picked up her virulently anti-Israel attitude. She opened her story with a description of West Bank refugee camps, none of which is visible on the route to the site. The entire article was about Israel's occupation of the Palestinians' land. Her highly biased story contained nothing new about the "situation" and precious little about what was really new—Adam's discoveries. And it was that article that most newspapers picked up and published. Adam's discovery was relegated to oblivion.

I'll grant that by peppering all his remarks with a maybe here, a possibly there, and a perhaps everywhere else, Adam made it seem as if there was nothing exciting to write about. Still, it was painful to see our work swept aside in favor of politically motivated polemics. Still, we did learn a lot from that news conference, and we became more determined than ever to keep a distance from anything political.

Much to his credit, Benny never advertised or exploited his support for Adam's academic work. He treated it with the same detachment any mayor would give a municipal project dedicated to cultural activities. If there was money in the till, Adam could have some. If not, he couldn't.

Benny knew that he could easily have taken advantage of the political implications of the findings at Ebal to further the cause of Gush Emunim, but he recognized that any move to capitalize on the discoveries would only jeopardize the perception of scientific legitimacy. He would do nothing to endanger that. Furthermore, in the years since I had introduced Benny and Adam to one another, the two had developed mutual respect and admiration—rare for people who come from their diametrically opposed backgrounds—and both men cherished their friendship.

Since the earliest days of the State of Israel, a struggle has been raging between Israel's secular nonreligious Jews and traditional Orthodox Jews. In recent years, that conflict has intensified, with each side challenging the legitimacy of the other. Both the observant and the secular groups are well aware of a famous story from the Second Temple Period. According to that story, the baseless hatred of two men led directly to the destruction of the Temple. Nevertheless, today's enemies—the observant and the secular—reserve harsher descriptions for one another than for the Palestinians who threaten the well-being and future of all of them.

In the op-ed pages of Israel's newspapers, this unbridled hatred plays itself out day after day. The various factions are wrestling for control of Israel's identity and future. I am quite sure that should the country collapse, it would not be at the hand of Arab armies. Internal strife and the crass political and religious leaders who fan the flames of anger will be responsible for Israel's fall.

By autumn of 1983, I was a regular visitor at Ein Shemer. As we strolled along the lanes of the Adam's kibbutz, my kipa, or yarmulke, attracted considerable attention. Some of the kibbutzniks regarded me as an enemy who had invaded their domain. Much to his credit, Adam never felt the need to justify or apologize for our friendship, and he never hesitated or was embarrassed to introduce me to his neighbors.

Our greatest problem was inadequate funding. I refer to this as "our" problem because I felt then—and I continue to feel even today—a strong need to help Adam with his projects. Benny had told me that it was becoming increasingly difficult to raise sufficient funds from the Council, so Adam and I knew that we had to develop other sources. Adam had hoped that the news conference would generate the kind of publicity that brings money, but such hopes evaporated quickly when we saw that the press preferred to present a story that featured long-suffering Palestinians rather than a fascinating excavation of remarkable implications.

As we approached the end of 1983, Adam and I started to consider the pros and cons of publishing an article about the excavations. Adam feared that it was much too early for him to write a scientific article. He was confident that future seasons would yield more fascinating and important discoveries, and he worried that a premature publication would invite unwelcome criticism and accusations that he had jumped the gun. He was partially right. Future seasons did yield great new discoveries, but he was wrong about what he expected from his academic colleagues. When and at what stage of the excavations he published, would make no difference at all. His report would have had exactly the same impact on the scientific community no matter how long he waited: his peers would express virtually no reaction at all.

Adam contacted the Israeli representative of *Biblical Archaeological Review* (*BAR*), whose popular style and approach addresses general rather than academic readers. The bimonthly, based in Washington, D.C., was founded and is edited by Hershel Shenks, an attorney who turned his hobby of biblical archaeology into a profitable publishing apparatus. Not long ago, Shenks was featured in headlines around the world: he had published the complete texts of the Dead Sea Scrolls without first getting permission from Israel's Department of Antiquities.

There has been criticism from certain segments of the academic community about *BAR*, but I have long admired the magazine. For the hundreds of thousands of laymen who have a deep and sincere interest in biblical research, *BAR* provides access to current research that is otherwise sequestered in the ivory towers of academia. The advisory board of *BAR*, comprising well-respected academic figures, maintains control over a tendency to promote sensationalist aspects of *BAR* articles. As a result, the magazine has grown by leaps and bounds, and ever-increasing numbers of the general public have access to the results of some of the most exciting research in this field.

Adam decided he would write an article for *BAR*, and I suggested that if he wrote it in Hebrew, I would be delighted to translate it into English. He gave me his first draft, and I told him that he would have to rewrite the beginning. He had neglected even to mention the survey as the research tool that had led to the discovery of the site. We submitted the manuscript to *BAR*, and it was returned to Adam with several questions and comments. The article finally appeared in the January 1985 issue, with the title presented in the form of a question mark: "Has Joshua's Altar Been Discovered at Mount Ebal?" The question mark had been Shenks's idea, Adam told me. The article generated a lot of interest and letters to the editor, but not much more than that. Few scholars would react to an article in a popular journal. Academicians will usually address only articles that are published in the professional literature of their discipline.

Nevertheless, one noted archaeologist, Aharon Kempinski, felt it necessary to respond to Adam's article, and he did so in a vengeful piece that appeared exactly one year later in January 1986. Kempinski was a lecturer at Tel Aviv University, where Adam had completed his advanced academic studies and obtained his doctorate in 1985. Adam had been one of his students. Kempinski had earned a reputation for being a bitter, outspoken critic of anyone whose opinion challenged his own. Also, his political views positioned him with Israel's far left. He visited Mount Ebal on October 27, 1982, and upon gaining the peak he exclaimed, "How lovely art thou, O Palestine!"

There can be no doubt about the political outlook of an Israeli archaeologist who describes the biblical area of Shechem and its environs as Palestine. Kempinski exhibited no qualms about his political opinions. Over the years, he had signed countless petitions, supporting Palestinians in every way and degrading everything Israeli. His attack on Adam in *BAR* was malignant and malicious, and it included a falsified description of the Ebal excavation.

Adam recalls that on the day of his one and only visit to the site, Kempinski circled the site for about ten minutes, making a few notes. He spoke not one word to Adam, his former student. He had come to the site with Benjamin Mazar and Amihai Mazar, Benjamin's nephew and a competent archaeologist in his own right.

Making no bones about his intentions, the title Kempinski gave his article was, "Joshua's Altar—An Iron Age Watchtower." Point by point, he presented Adam as a charlatan. Kempinski offered a series of arguments that aimed not only to question the correctness of Adam's identification of the site, but also to discredit Adam as a scientist. He deliberately misrepresented various facets of our discoveries, suggesting interpretations that were grounded not in the facts of the excavations but only in his own fertile imagination.

Although Adam took the opportunity to rebut Kempinski's challenge in the same issue of the magazine, it is Kempinski's article that stands out, and it is Kempinski's article that is remembered by the collective academic community. I was deeply shaken after a conversation I had with a noted biblical scholar who told me that he saw no reason even to read Adam's rebuttal once he saw that Kempinski had nullified Adam's work.

In his rebuttal, Adam made no mention at all of the wickedest aspect of Kempinski's attack. I don't know whether that omission was oversight on Adam's part or if Adam deliberately made a politic decision not to call Kempinski a liar. Nevertheless, Kempinski did worse than lie; he presented a forgery.

Amihai Mazar had been excavating an Iron Age site at Giloh in southern Jerusalem. That site has several characteristics in common with the Ebal site. Those similarities include an outer wall and what looks like an inner enclosure. The inner wall of the Giloh site, however, contains houses. Kempinski took a drawing of the Giloh site and erased the houses in order to make the Giloh sketch look like the two sets of walls at Ebal. There were, of course, no houses at Ebal within the wall perimeters. In his desperation to destroy Adam's credibility, Kempinski actually falsified the diagram of Giloh excavation, making it appear to represent the Ebal site, and he presented the doctored picture to *BAR!*

Israeli television is controlled by the government. Recently, steps have been taken to loosen the governmental hold on this powerful medium, and even privately owned cable TV has been introduced. However, even when the Likud governments of Menachem Begin and Yitzhak Shamir ran the country, the popular

News of the Week, which airs on Friday nights, was controlled exclusively by left-wing editors and reporters. On Friday evening, March 31, 1984, the "News of the Week" broadcast a feature about the Ebal excavations. Because I wouldn't turn on the television on the Sabbath, I didn't see the program, but a few days later, I watched the tape Adam had made of it. And what I saw made my blood boil.

In the beginning of the program, Adam made a brief presentation about the site, accompanying his statement with photos of the site. After Adam, viewers heard the from Binyamin Zedakah, a prominent leader of the Samaritan community, and the late Anwar Nusseibah, a Palestinian who had been a minister in the Jordanian government and whose son, Dr. Seri Nusseibah, is considered one of the leading Palestinians in the West Bank.

The Samaritan version of the Pentateuch differs from the standard Jewish Masoretic text in some 6,000 ways. Few reputable scholars maintain that the Samaritan text preceded the Jewish text. The Samaritan population was concentrated in the region of Shechem and Samaria. According to II Kings 17:24, the Assyrians conducted regular transfers of populations with the hope that removing nations from their home territories would expedite the destruction of their nationalistic impulses and any desire to revolt. The Assyrians exiled the Israelites from Samaria and uprooted populations of nations from five places in Mesopotamia—Babylon, Cuthah, Avva, Hamath, and Sepharvaim—and relocated them to the cities of Samaria. According to the biblical account, lions attacked the newcomers, who were quite sure that the attacks had been brought about on account of their cultic practices. The Assyrian king, hearing of new residents' plight, sent in an Israelite priest whom he had previously exiled to Assyria. Setting the priest up in Beth-el, the king had him instruct the immigrants in the local cultic ways. Apparently, his efforts were successful. The lions headed in other directions, looking for different ways to satisfy their hunger. The new residents of Samaria became known as the Samaritans. The Bible reports that the Samaritans kept many of their old pagan customs, and as a result, Jewish animosity toward the Samaritans continued for hundreds of years. This ill will reached its zenith when the Talmud expressly forbade sharing even a glass of water with a Samaritan, lest that act lead to a personal relationship.

Two of the Samaritans' changes to the biblical text are relevant to the story of Ebal. First, they added a sentence to the traditional version of the Ten

Commandments, explaining that the First Commandment, "I am the Lord," should not be counted as one of the Commandments—that it is only an introductory verse. The sentence they added and designated as their Tenth Commandment, is, "Three times a year shall all your males come to the place that He will choose, Mount Moriah, [which is] Mount Gerizim." The same verse—without the mention of Mount Moriah or Mount Gerizim—is found in Deuteronomy of the Jewish text. Moriah is the site of Abraham's binding and near-sacrifice of his son Isaac. Jewish tradition identifies Mount Moriah as the Temple Mount in Jerusalem.

The Jews, led by Ezra and Nehemiah, returned from the Babylonian exile that followed the destruction of the First Temple. They would not allow the Samaritans to participate in rebuilding Jerusalem and the Temple. Consequently, the Samaritans built their own sanctuary on Mount Gerizim, and to accommodate the identification of Mount Gerizim as the central holy site, they altered a number of relevant biblical texts.

Furthermore, they changed Deuteronomy 27, substituting Mount Gerizim for Mount Ebal as the site of the altar for the ceremony of the blessings and the curses. Adam's identification of the Ebal altar as the altar mentioned in Deuteronomy 27 undermines the very foundations of the Samaritan religion and indicates that their biblical text—not the Masoretic text—is false.

It was no wonder then that when their foremost spokesman, Benyamin Zedaka, was interviewed on Israeli television, he went to great lengths to discredit the find and, indeed, Adam personally. Of course, the television interviewer failed to present the historical background. When most viewers don't have even the foggiest notion about the differences between Samaritans and Jews and the textual differences in their respective Bibles, such omissions are certainly significant. For viewers whose knowledge was limited to what they were seeing and hearing on this program, it appeared that the dispute was simply a question of one man's word against another's, and it had a devastating effect on the apparent veracity of Adam's claims.

It's no wonder the Samaritans had challenged Adam's findings. Adam's research, which had clearly substantiated the biblical description, was undermining basic tenets of Samaritan belief. The picture grew even cloudier for the Samaritans a few years after that broadcast. Adam called and asked me to stop at his home so that he could show me something interesting. When I arrived, he presented me with a scientific paper from, of all places, the University of Baghdad. The paper described a type cuneiform that decorates the base of certain pottery vessels. The pottery dated to the seventh century BCE, the period during which the Bible says the Samaritans were brought to the land of Israel. Adam reminded me that exactly the same sort of writing appears on the same sort of vessels that had been unearthed in 43 sites of his survey. I found it more than "interesting" to read that the vessels described in the Baghdad paper had been discovered in three of the five cities mentioned in II Kings 17:24. This evidence offers strong support to the biblical version and challenges the Samaritans' claim that they are the descendents of the tribes of Joseph and priestly families.

When Anwar Nusseibah had his opportunity to make his case before the television audience, Nusseibah, who represented a Palestinian point of view, had the audacity to claim that Ebal had been a Hivvite site. In Genesis 34, the Bible describes the slaughter of the Hivvites by Jacob's sons Simeon and Levi following the rape of their sister Dinah. Nowhere in the archaeological history of Israel has there been a discovery that is identified as Hivvite, one of the seven Canaanite nations that God had instructed the Israelites to conquer. There simply is no scientific evidence that supports Nesseibah's claim that Ebal was a Hivvite site.

Like the Samaritans, the Arabs have made their own adjustments to biblical history, aiming, as much as possible, to deny a historical connection between Israel and what they call Palestine. The Koran, for example, has rewritten the story of Abraham's aborted sacrifice of his son Isaac. Instead of Isaac, the Koran says that Abraham had attempted to offer Ishmael, the patriarch of Moslems, in sacrifice. When Arabs settled in Israel, they changed the longtime names of local sites, especially those whose names were significant in biblical history. They excised El, one of the biblical names of God, from Beth-el, renaming it Beit'in. Yizrael, Hebrew for "Jezreel," went through a similar linguistic circumcision, becoming Zar'in. These are only two of many, many examples.

Nusseibah's "reassessment" of the historical origins of the Ebal site, was simply another episode in the Arabs' 1,500-year-old tradition of recreating the past. Notwithstanding Nusseibah's complete lack of credentials or authority in the fields of archaeology and ancient history, the television interviewer allowed Nusseibah to present his baseless version as a creditable theory.

And for at least the next decade, Israeli television has given no further coverage to Adam's work at Mount Ebal. Adam was able to arouse the media's attention only with his discovery of an artifact at an Iron Age site north of Ebal in 1987, four years later. At that site, Adam had found a clay penis, which seems to have broken from an Israelite statue that dates back to the 12th century BCE. The piece is remarkable in that it provides evidence of circumcision at a very early period of Israelite history. Most scientists had set the introduction of Israelite circumcision at a much later date. As a result of that find, Adam was invited to appear on a very popular news-magazine program. The interviewer, pandering to the tastes and interests of the viewing public couldn't be bothered to discuss the history of circumcision, and the sly double-entendres that peppered the interviewer's questions did little to enhance Adam's status as a serious archaeologist.

So none of Adam's public relations opportunities bore fruit: not the publication of the article in *BAR*, not the press conference, and not even the television report generated the funding Adam needed to further his research. I had invested so much physical and emotional energy into the Mount Ebal project that I shared Adam's agony. We were both beginning to give up hope of even one more season of excavations. Then, all of a sudden, in the spring of 1984, the future seemed to brighten.

One Friday afternoon during the Passover holiday, as I was on my way to pick up a few things at the Shavei Shomron grocery store, two large BMWs drove up alongside me. At the time, the sight of any BMW in our small town was enough to raise eyebrows. And to see two brand-new, top-of-the-line BMWs was simply extraordinary. My curiosity getting the best of me, I stood there, empty shopping bags in my hands, transfixed.

Both cars pulled over and the passengers and drivers climbed out of their cars. One man, tall, middle-aged, and tanned, approached me with a friendly smile. He introduced himself as David Cohen and explained that he had brought some English friends of his for a tour of Samaria. He himself was a well-known, Israeli-born industrialist. His friends, he explained, were an English family—a grandfather, his two daughters with their husbands, as well as some of his grandchildren. The grandfather, it turned out, was a great philanthropist who has a long history as a supporter of Jewish and Israeli causes. The daughters and their families had recently immigrated to Israel from England. They had settled in Herzlia Pituach, the Beverly Hills of Israel.

As they emerged from the cars, stretching their arms and legs, I could see that they had come from another world. Rather than wearing the jeans, t-shirt, and sandals that were the uniform of most residents of Shavei Shomron, or Ein Shemer for that matter, these men and women were dressed in what high-end couturiers term, "casual wear." I looked at them and thought to myself, what are these peacocks doing in this town of drab, brown sparrows? Despite their elegance, I found them far from ostentatious. Still, I couldn't help thinking that just one of the wristwatches those people were sporting could finance one or more very intensive seasons of excavations. David, the one Israeli in the party, was dressed in simpler clothing—a plain white shirt and slacks.

David asked me for directions to the town's computer factory. At the time, our factory produced software, as well as computer parts. I accompanied them to the facility, but because of the holiday, it had closed early, and everyone was gone for the day.

Opportunity, as the saying goes, knocks only once, and I was doing some fast thinking. Here was a chance for me to help Adam. I decided that I wouldn't let the visitors leave without my making an attempt to interest them in our archaeological excavations. It was 1:00 p.m., and I had nothing better to do, so I suggested that they might like a guided tour to the nearby Arab village of Sebastia, which houses a national archaeological park with impressive ruins. David, who was feeling uncomfortable about having hauled his friends on a pointless excursion, found the idea especially pleasing.

Sebastos is Greek for "august" or "exalted," and King Herod had named Sebastia in honor of Augustus Caesar. Omri, Ahab's father, had built the city, which was originally named Samaria. It was the last capital of the Northern Kingdom of Israel, and it was from there that the Assyrians had deported the Israelites. Excavations conducted from 1929 through 1935 had uncovered a palace built by Ahab, other Israelite ruins dating back to about 800 BCE, a Roman theater, a basilica, a hippodrome, and additional features typical of Roman cities. Built on a hilltop, the remains of the ancient city afford an excellent view for miles around. During periods of good visibility—especially spring and winter—one can easily see the Mediterranean Sea, 25 miles away.

I pulled out all the stops. I had guided numerous groups around this site, and I did everything I could think of to stimulate the interest of these people. I escorted them on an exciting trip through some 3,000 years of Sebastia's history. About a half-hour into our tour, I stopped at a vantage point from which the military antennae at the peak of Ebal were clearly visible. Not willing to let their attention wander even for a moment, I asked them to stretch out and then seat themselves on the ancient Roman stones. Lowering my voice to a conspiratorial level, I leaned toward them and pointed to Ebal.

Recounting the biblical narration of the blessings and the curses, I gradually introduced them to the story of our excavations, climaxing with the details of the day Adam and I recognized the similarity of the altar at Ebal to the Mishnah's depiction of the Second Temple's altar. They were spellbound. The two brothers-in-law, Frank Green and Lenny Maxwell, were thrilled. Frank, an architect, expressed an eagerness to visit the site. I told him that quite frankly, it was difficult to visit the site but I'd ask Adam whether we could arrange a special tour. Handing me a card with his phone number, Frank said that he'd be in England for a while and asked me to phone in a month's time.

The tour was a huge success. Everyone, especially David, thanked me, and as they drove off, heading back to Herzliya Pituach, I ran home to phone Adam.

I have a tendency to be extremely enthusiastic, and this occasion certainly merited all the excitement I could muster. My description of my encounter with the English family was exuberant, to say the least, and even Adam was ready to admit that they were the kind of people who should be encouraged to support the project.

A few weeks later, Adam called to tell me that CNN had asked him to escort its Israeli correspondent, Jay Bushinsky, along with a camera crew, to the Ebal site. We agreed that since visits to the West Bank location weren't that easy to arrange, Adam would invite the two English couples to join the tour he'd be arranging for the CNN people.

Even during the period that preceded the intifada, it was not so easy to get to the site. Adam and I were unwilling to leave anything up to chance. What if Frank and Lenny took a wrong turn? They could end up in an isolated Arab village, where they might be given a less than friendly welcome. I arranged to meet their car at Tulkarm, near the entrance to the West Bank. From there, they would follow me.

The day of our excursion was a perfectly glorious day in May. We drove through the military base and made our way over the dirt path that took us to a clearing above the site. Leaving the cars there, we gingerly climbed down the steep hill and over the rough footpath to the outskirts of the site.

CNN was already there: two cameramen and Bushinsky, who had brought a friend of his, Micha Bar-Am, one of the best-known photographers in Israel. I spoke with Bar-Am, whose response was disconcertingly aloof. Only later did I learn that politically he is associated with Israel's left wing and that he makes no secret of his impatience with biblical and historical excavations on the West Bank. Bushinsky, a seasoned reporter, had worked for many important media outlets, and he was a well-known figure among the foreign journalists in Israel. Like many of the reporters I've met, he was very cool and reserved. He made it quite clear that he would be much happier meeting with a politician in a comfortable office or in the lobby of one of the better hotels in Tel Aviv or Jerusalem.

As the cameras rolled, Adam launched into his explanation of what we had found at the site. Bushinsky didn't bother to ask questions. I stood near the cameraman, speaking only when he asked me a question about the excavations. Adam and I had worked out the best sequence for showing the site to visitors.

We always started the presentation by drawing visitors' attention to the panoramic view from the top of Ebal. It is, after all, among the most breathtaking views in Israel. On that particularly clear day, we were able to see snow-capped Mount Hermon in the northern tip of the Golan Heights. Lowering our eyes, we could see the Gilboa range, where the Philistines killed King Saul and his son Jonathan. Looking east, to the right, we could see the lush Far'ah Valley almost to the Jordan. Above the valley, we could easily make out the mountains across the Jordan, and the peak of Jebel Kabir, with the town of Elon Moreh behind it. Swinging south and to the right, we could see the Dajan Valley, which took its name from the Hebrew *dagan,* which means "wheat." The Mishnah reports that the early harvest of wheat from this valley was offered at the Temple during Passover as the Omer offering. (Leviticus 23:9-14.) Almost everything we could see had biblical and historic significance, and Adam spoke briefly about each point of interest.

Once everyone had taken in the spectacular view, Adam began to explain the survey, which encompassed almost the entire area visible from the site. He described the problems of identifying the main central structure, and it was at this point that Bushinsky finally evinced signs of interest. But when Adam produced a professionally drawn rendition of the site and set it next to the drawing of the Second Temple's altar that appears in the Mishnah, Bushinsky's eyes grew big and round. Although he didn't say a word, I could tell that he was really impressed. Micha Bar-Am, however, had brought his preconceived notions with him, and he diligently ignored Adam and his presentation.

For dramatic effect, Adam always concluded tours of the site at the base of the ramp that leads to the top of the altar and from which the face of the altar is completely visible. At this point of the tour, Adam opened a Bible to Deuteronomy 27, placed it in Lenny's hands, and asked him to read the sentences that describe the ceremony of the blessings and the curses and God's command that the Israelites build an altar in Mount Ebal. Lenny and the rest of his family were overcome with emotion. Frank, Lenny, and their wives were so moved by what they had seen that they remained silent for several moments, gazing at the altar in speechless wonder.

Actually, everyone who has had this experience finds it quite moving. Two of Israel's military chiefs-of-staff, Moshe Levi and former Prime Minister Ehud Barak, have visited the site. These tough army men, both products of atheist kibbutzim, were nevertheless unable to keep their hands and voices from trembling as they read the biblical sentences aloud.

To our enormous disappointment, CNN has never aired a program based on the tour we gave to Bushinsky and the others. Still, our other guests were impressed that CNN had sent a crew to the site. To them, CNN's presence bestowed a certain credibility on our work, and within a few days, Frank phoned to invite Adam and me to meet with him at his home. By this time, Adam, too, was becoming enthusiastic about the possibilities these people offered.

Before we made the trip, Adam and I met to prepare a financial statement—a sort of business plan—detailing what we'd need in order to complete the excavations and prepare the site for public visits. Without exaggerating any of the expenses, we determined that we'd need $350,000. That astronomical, unimaginable sum was certainly within reach of our newfound friends.

What was my "stake" in all this? The answer is very simple. My fondest dream is one day to be in charge of the site when it is open to visitors. I want to spend every single day of my life there. Adam supported my dream wholeheartedly, and as the site's lead archaeologist, he would have a strong say about any decisions concerning its future.

One evening the following week, the two of us met outside Frank's home. As we rang the bell, I noticed that the house was protected by an extremely sophisticated alarm system—good enough for a bank, jewelry store, or even a top-secret government installation. The door would open only if somebody punched the correct combination of keys on the golden number pad. Frank greeted us at the door and led us to a large study, furnished with a huge, rectangular table that was surrounded by a number of elaborate easy chairs. Up until then, I had seen such furnishings only in really lavish Manhattan office suites. It was astonishing to find such a room in Israel. But Herzlia Pituach, where Frank lived, is like any fancy neighborhood around the world—distinctly detached from the lives of the rest of the population.

Before sitting down, I tried to take in as much of the room as possible. The walls were covered with paintings by artists whose works adorn the world's most famous museums. I'm sure I am not exaggerating when I say that for the price of those paintings, Frank could have supported every archaeological project in Israel for at least a century.

Frank and Lenny had invited three of their friends, as well as David, to sit in on this meeting. In front of each of chair, there was already a yellow writing pad and a sharpened pencil. Adam and I exchange a glance that said, things were indeed looking up.

I presented copies of the business plan to the five men, and, as Adam and I had planned, I answered all questions about our numbers. Frank suggested a simple and straightforward plan. He had decided to form and chair a committee that would undertake to raise funds for the project. Lenny, a wonderful talker and salesman, would recruit potential donors, and each of the others would coordinate media, accounting, legal matters, and other concerns that might arise.

Not for a single moment did Adam or I doubt the sincerity of their intentions. It was clear to us that Frank and Lenny, newly arrived from England and semiretired with lots of time on their hands, found our project exciting and worthy of their support and efforts.

Almost immediately, Lenny asked us about the site's legal status. Archaeologists apply to Israel's Department of Antiquities for permits that protect their excavations. Such a permit, which is renewable for each season of a site's excavation, enjoins the owner of the land from making any changes to it—no plowing or planting—for the duration of the excavation. Should excavations cease, a decree from the Department of Antiquities declaring the site an antiquity allows for excavations in future generations and prohibits the landowner from ever using it for agricultural or any other purposes.

Lenny pointed out that such a decree would be a prerequisite for gaining control of the site for public visits, and he asked that we immediately arrange for one. He noted that it was senseless for the committee even to contemplate serious efforts before we had secured a decree. We saw the logic of his argument and agreed that we would do everything possible to achieve that goal as soon as possible. Of course, we had no idea that this tiny technicality would be the source of sheer misery for years to come.

I prodded Adam to file his application with the Department of Antiquities. Itzik Magen, Staff Officer of Antiquities, headed the West Bank operation of the Department of Antiquities. Government agencies that serve the West Bank and Gaza were under the auspices of two bosses: the Israeli government agency with which they were affiliated and what is known as the Civilian Administration of the West Bank and Gaza. The Civilian Administration is a military apparatus that provides civilian services in the territories that are under Israel's control.

Anyone who has two bosses, actually has no boss at all. And Itzik, with his iron-strong will, had no interest in accommodating Adam. The two of them already had a history of disagreements, and Adam, also a stubborn individualist, found it painful to ask Itzik for favors. The few times Adam had lowered himself to ask, he'd got nothing but broken promises.

Consequently, when Adam submitted his letter to Itzik requesting that the site be declared an antiquity, neither of us expected quick turnaround. Nevertheless, we did have some expectation of hearing from him within a reasonable time span. We were wrong.

At the end of two months, when we hadn't heard so much as one word from Itzik, I decided to intercede. I spoke with Benny Katzover. As the region's top political honcho, Benny had no authority over the granting of such permits, but he promised to call Freddy Zach, a general who was in charge of the Civilian Administration of the West Bank. True to his word, Benny managed to arrange a meeting. The meeting, at which time a decision would be made, would involve Freddy, Itzik, Adam, and a number of other functionaries. It was to take place at the beginning of September 1984, a full three months after Adam's letter to Itzik. Because of a spate of terrorist activity in August, however, that meeting had to be rescheduled. Zach had more pressing things to do than climb up to Ebal and mediate the ego problems of archaeologists.

Apprising Frank of the situation, I apologized for Israel's convoluted bureaucracy and begged for his patience. Lenny, the salesman, asked me to schedule a tour of the site during the holiday of Succoth in mid-October. His group of fifteen people was the perfect size for a minibus. We agreed to make it an all-day trip, including visits to several other sites in the area.

The morning of our excursion, I arrived at Lenny's house with the minibus and its driver, Zev, a sociable, outgoing guy who knew the site, having taxied our volunteers back and forth during excavation seasons. One by one, Lenny introduced me to his friends who would be joining us for the day. Then, taking me aside for a moment, he told me a few details about each of them. They were all among England's most philanthropic Jews, and all of them, sharing a strong affinity for Israel, were grateful that Lenny had invited them to join him on this outing. Lenny was pleased when I commended him on his having done a first-class sales job. It was clear that the guests understood that at some point in the near future, Lenny would be expecting their financial participation in this venture.

By 8:15 a.m., we were on our way. Once everyone was seated in the minibus, I started to talk, stopping only to catch my breath, accept questions, and laugh at Zev's wisecracks. Everyone was attentive and involved, and the questions people asked were thoughtful and appropriate. I had chosen a route from Herzlia Pituach to Samaria that would take us past most of Samaria's Jewish settlements. We managed to avoid seeing Arab towns until we were in the vicinity of Nablus.

Because I wanted to avoid all unnecessary delays, I had contacted the military in advance of our trip and arranged for our quick passage through the army base at the summit of Ebal. I was pleased that everything was proceeding so smoothly.

As the bus made the slow climb to the top of Mount Ebal, I started my description of the general area. My presentation followed Adam's model, but, as usual, I added my own emotional point of view. I could tell that every person on the minibus was excited by my narrative, which emphasized the connections between the finds at the site and the biblical texts.

At the climax of the tour I handed a Bible to one of the men and asked him to read the relevant biblical verses while the rest of us stood gazing at the site. Of course, this bit of drama always elicited the same results. And that group was particularly engaged: I had to prod them to leave. They were enthralled.

Back in the bus, we descended Ebal to Joseph's Tomb, which is located on the eastern side of Nablus. As part of my description of the site's history, I told our guests that 1,600 years before the birth of the Palestine Liberation Organization, the rabbis of the Talmud taught that should gentiles claim that the land of Israel belongs to them and assert that Jews were merely foreign conquerors, we Jews are obligated to remind them of no fewer than three sites that our forefathers purchased for cold cash. Those three sites belong to the children of Israel—forever. Abraham bought the Cave of the Machpela in Hebron for the burial of his wife, Sarah. Even though King David had conquered Jerusalem, he insisted on paying the Jebusites for the land that is the site of the Temple Mount. And according to the Bible, Joseph had instructed the Israelites to take his body from Egypt and return it to Canaan. Moses made sure to transport Joseph's bones to the land of Israel, and he passed the task of the burial to his successor, Joshua, who purchased land for the burial of Joseph's remains. Despite all that, the Arabs have pronounced claims to each of those three sites.

Upon our return to Lenny's house, a number of the guests approached me with checkbooks in hand. They had been so impressed by the Ebal site, that right then and there, they were ready to hand over substantial contributions. I was pretty much swooning with delight until Lenny threw a wrench into the works. Speaking as the voice of reason, Lenny informed the men and women that Adam was still contending with bureaucratic arcana that had so far impeded the award of a decree establishing the site as an official antiquity. As such, Lenny explained, contributions were premature. He assured them that he would welcome their contributions once those obstacles had been cleared. The checkbooks disappeared into pockets, heartfelt thanks were offered, and Lenny invited Zev and me to join him for a drink.

Although I was striving to mask my disappointment, I'm sure that it was as obvious as could be. Lenny's caution was certainly warranted, but knowing that we faced an inescapable series of inevitable delays, I fretted that time would only dampen the enthusiasm of our would-be benefactors.

We had scheduled a new date for the authorities' official visit. But when the late October date arrived, once again urgent matters necessitated another postponement. I nearly wept when Benny's secretary informed me of this latest delay. I was miserable at the thought of having to explain once again to Frank and Lenny that we simply had not yet managed to get the critical approvals.

Just as we had feared, apologies and explanations have a very short half-life. In mid-November, Frank summoned me to his home and informed me that he would be discontinuing his efforts on our behalf. Looking at the situation from his point of view, I could appreciate that he was acting sensibly. Nevertheless, I was devastated.

I believed that it was quite possible that I would simply shrivel up and die. I liked Frank. He had always been straightforward with us. His heart was in the right place, but, unfortunately for Adam and me, so was his head. His conscience and common sense would not allow him to enter a project that was uncertain, and he was unwilling to permit his friends to contribute money to a lost cause. I'm sure that he sensed my acute disappointment, but we did part on good terms, and I promised to keep him well informed of our progress.

Five weeks after suffering this terrible setback, I had a phone call from a prominent Washington, D.C. rabbi, who had seen the *BAR* article. When the rabbi expressed his interest in seeing the site, I gladly arranged a tour for him and his wife. I had had a letter from my sister, who had informed me that the rabbi was one of the most influential rabbis in the Washington metropolitan area—possibly in the entire United States. She believed that if he wanted to, he could easily raise money for our projects.

Taking him through my by-now rote explanation of the site, I nevertheless elicited the same routine reaction. He was thrilled and overwhelmed. Despite his enthusiasm, however, he had no interest in helping us. I could see that it must be a lot easier to find generous contributors to projects that involve university or hospital buildings. Donors are gratified to have their names emblazoned on golden plaques for eternity. Finding contributions for basic research is infinitely more difficult. The rabbi explained that he would be retiring soon and, therefore, he was in no position to undertake new endeavors. Although, I felt like choking him for wasting my time and effort, I smiled and returned him to his Jerusalem apartment.

Finally, one week after my fruitless tour with the rabbi, on January 1, 1985, our meeting with Freddy, Itzik, Adam, Benny, and the rest of the responsible players took place. As Adam was showing Freddy the site, Itzik made quite a show of being bored and uninterested. When Adam spotted him starting to climb the ramp that leads to the top of the altar, Adam interrupted his monologue and ordered Itzik to get off the fragile structure. During the awkward moment it took Itzik to get off his high horse and the ramp, everyone stood silent. Adam simply continued his presentation, and Freddy, visibly impressed, instructed Itzik to process our request immediately and without delay.

The final decree reached Adam two weeks later, signed and sealed. The moment I heard, I phoned Frank, and he invited me to stop by at his home. Proudly, I presented the documents and the *BAR* article for his examination. To no avail. It was too late. Frank had lost interest, and nothing we could do or say could change his mind.

I phoned Adam and told him that we wouldn't get a cent from Frank. We were in big trouble. I had injudiciously counted on Frank's beneficence and, considering it to be virtually a done deal, I'd made some purchases for the previous season's excavations, paying for them out of the budget of my town's field school. Such expenditures should have had the approval of the school's directors—a three-man panel of fellow townspeople. I had feared that because of their narrow vision, the directors would not approve the expenditures. I figured that the limitations they had imposed on their thinking would have blinded them to the importance of the excavations. And I was certain they'd be incapable of understanding the potential profits our town might enjoy when the site opened to the public. So, acting unilaterally and without authorization, I simply spent $7,000. Neither of us was in any position to repay the school.

The situation was worse than embarrassing. My wife, who had long criticized what she considered to be my overinvolvement with Adam, redoubled her criticisms. Life was becoming very much unbearable, and I was desperate to straighten out the financial mess I'd created.

After some discussion, Adam and I agreed to approach Michael Fox, Frank's legal counsel. Michael, head of one of Israel's most prestigious law firms, agreed to meet with us at his Tel Aviv office. We explained our problem, explaining that Frank's enthusiasm had led us to believe that we could count on his financial support. We had kept our part of the bargain, albeit belatedly. Still, the delay had certainly been due to circumstances beyond our control. Michael agreed to visit the site with us, so that he could get a clear picture and assure himself that we had told him the whole story. As always, we made our routine presentation; as always, Michael reacted just as everyone else had. A reprint of the article in *BAR* didn't hurt, either.

He met with Frank and after some cajoling, Frank made a very generous donation that more than covered the debt to our field school. Adam immediately repaid the debt, but the cumulative weight of all the problems associated with my involvement in the project had crushed my spirit.

Since our earliest interactions with Frank and Lenny, I had been toying with a new approach. It was impossible to ignore the remarkable and inevitable reaction everyone had upon visiting the site. The more I thought about that, the more I was convinced that the only feasible approach would be for us to open the site to the public. We could then apply at least some of the proceeds to financing further scientific endeavors. Israel has a class of public parks that is authorized to charge entrance fees. Such well-known archaeological sites as Massada and Caeserea are under the jurisdiction of the National Parks Authority (NPA). I phoned and arranged a meeting with Motke Porat, a retired general, who was the director-general of the NPA.

Porat received me in his Tel Aviv office at the Kirya, a large complex of military and civilian government offices. He heard me out and agreed to pay a visit to the site along with several NPA directors. His notably unbureaucratic approach impressed me as extraordinary for an Israeli official, and true to his word, he and his colleagues did visit the site. And, as usual, even the most skeptical members of his party were impressed.

During our second meeting, at which I had hoped to map out the practical steps we'd need to follow, Porat told me a story that left me feeling very sad. It turns out that he, himself, had no control over the excessively bureaucratic procedures that must precede the opening of an NPA park. And, he added, we could expect the process to last some five to ten years.

Porat suggested that I turn to the local Regional Council, which was legally able to achieve the same end with less red tape. Perhaps, he said, our Regional Council would be less encumbered by time-consuming bureaucratic procedures. He kindly told me that his door would always be open to me if I had need of advice, and he added that he would ask his staff to instruct me on any phase of the operation I wanted. I thanked him gratefully, and set out to formulate a plan.

With my educational background in hotel administration, I was able to prepare most of the plan on my own. But the plan was not enough. I turned to my friend Isaac Westman for advice. I had met Isaac, a Tel Aviv lawyer who specializes in commercial law, through his daughter who had been a soldier assigned to our field school. When he visited her in our town, he and I had had a long conversation about my immigration to Israel. When I described my memory of the captured Jordanian tanks being driven from Jerusalem just after the Six-Day War, he laughed because he had been in one of those tanks.

Isaac and I met at his office near Ibn Gvirol Street, an area whose ground-level apartments—much to the chagrin of the buildings' residents—had been converted into offices. Isaac is a few years older than I and several inches shorter, and he carries a pot belly that mars his otherwise very handsome appearance. His office phone rings continually, and our meeting was interrupted more than a few times. He had warned me to expect that, and he had promised that he would hear me out completely. He had no difficulty resuming the continuously interrupted conversation, and I could tell by his razor-sharp questions that he didn't miss a single word.

I began by describing Adam's project and how I had come to get involved in it. Then, not dreaming in my worst nightmares that more of the same was on the way, I recited the entire litany of disappointments we had endured. Finally, I presented my idea of turning the site into a park. To put my plan into action, we'd need to formulate a contractual agreement with the Regional Council, and I had come to him for advice on how to proceed. Isaac asked me to get answers to a number of technical questions, and he gave me the guidelines for preparing a business plan that could be translated into a contract. Fully aware of my inability to pay legal fees, Isaac told me that he found our project so interesting that it would provide a pleasant break from the typically mundane tasks of commercial law.

Between deep drags on ever-present cigarettes, Isaac directed an army of secretaries and junior assistants, conducted business over the phone, and managed to give me invaluable advice—all from his huge leather swivel chair. I admit that at first I was offended and irritated by his frenetic style, but in time I learned that it was certainly worth my while—and worth far more than I could ever pay for such incredibly useful advice—to adjust my expectations.

He drew up a contract for me to present to the Regional Council. If the council agreed, it would first secure the permits necessary to create an archaeological park at the Ebal site and then lease me the site. The agreement would not require any financial commitment from the council, and I offered even to arrange for the planning. I asked only for the council's permission to act on its behalf, proceeding subject to its approval of the plans and contractual clauses.

I met with Benny, and he agreed to let me present the proposed contract to a full session of the council. As most of the council had visited the site during our excavations, I already knew most of the members personally. The meeting went smoothly, and when the council agreed to my plan in principle, I set out to complete the package and draw up the rest of the plans.

In Israel, most commercial ventures depend on some kind of government funding. But because I have such low regard for government bureaucracy, I was determined to avoid dependency on government agencies. Rather than ask for public funding, I intended to find private investments to back the project, and I was confident that with Isaac Westman's help and advice, I would have no problem doing so.

I went back to Porat at the NPA, and he gave me the names of a number of architects with whom his agency works. After meeting with each of them, I elected to work with Philip Bogod, a French-born resident of Jerusalem. I was most impressed with the magnificent planning he had done for several ancient sites. He came to the site to meet Adam, and he was suitably awed by what we had found. It would have been a perfect day except for the marked increase in military and police activity that we passed as we drove through Nablus on our way back to Jerusalem. That evening, as I listened to the news, I learned that while Adam,

Philip, and I were making plans up on the hill, terrorists were murdering Hikmat El-Masri, the mayor of Nablus, on the steps of his city hall. El-Masri, the son of a prominent Arab family and a very proud Palestinian, could never be described as a friend of Israel. But his Western education and manners were apparently loathsome to a group of fringe terrorists who managed to murder him and escape capture— even though the police station is directly across the street from the city hall.

I had warned Philip that he could not expect to be paid until after the plans had been received. He said he understood and drew up some sketches. (Apparently he did get impatient, however. A while later he billed the council for his services.) With Adam's approval, I assembled the package that the council had requested. Both of us agreed that we did not want to ask for public funding. Because he and Itzik, who controlled the financial faucets for West Bank projects, didn't get along, Adam knew that he should expect little if any help from the Department of Antiquities.

I knew that if we approached investors in the United States, we'd have a much better chance of raising the money we needed to develop and prepare the site for public access. Furthermore, I realized that it would be worthwhile getting advice about the Ebal project from my childhood friends who had experience in such relevant fields as law and entrepreneurial business. Five years had passed since my last visit, so a trip back to the United States was long overdue. And, quite frankly, I knew that I needed a break. The project was a source of relentless turmoil, and it was exacting an emotional toll. I was growing increasingly irritable, impatient, intolerant, and intolerable.

I decided to schedule a visit to family and friends in New York. As I was doing some last minute packing the night before my departure, I was interrupted by a disturbing phone call. The long arm of Kempinski was once again stretching out to damage Adam's prestige and reputation. Debbie Hershman, one of Kempinski's students, was a reporter for *Koteret Rashit,* a weekly, left-wing news magazine. She had heard that we were trying to turn the Ebal site into a tourist attraction, and she had set out to write an exposé that would "reveal" Adam's connections with Gush Emunim.

To this day, I have no idea who had told her that she should talk to me, but she insisted that we had to meet for an interview. I told her that I was going abroad the next day, but I would answer her questions on the phone. When I said that I was indeed working on a plan to have the Ebal site opened to the public, her excitement was almost embarrassing. But when I explained to her that the project was to be privately funded and would not be connected to Gush Emunim or any other political movement, her enthusiasm cooled. She didn't believe this for one minute, and she tried to browbeat me for incriminating details. I quickly tired of this tack and told her that it was none of her business. The article appeared six weeks later, and it was a killer.

Its Hebrew title, *Hazevach Veharevach,* "The Sacrifices and the Profits," rhymes. And in any language it is libelous. The article, insinuating devilish machinations of Gush Emunim, suggested that Adam had become a—willing or unwilling—pawn of the "insanely religious right-wing," who wanted to create yet another sacred spot on the West Bank, adding salt to the wounds of the long-suffering Arabs. The reporter had, of course, quoted Kempinski, denigrating Adam and comparing his work to that of Heinrich Schliemann, whose excavations of Troy are in disrepute. In ordinary times, the two-page article would have raised quite a stir. However, timing of its publication doomed it to left-wing oblivion. In the same issue, *Koteret Rashit* had blown open one of the biggest scandals in Israel's history.

Some time before, four Arab terrorists had hijacked a public bus traveling from Tel Aviv to Ashekelon. The terrorists had killed one female passenger who happened to have been a soldier. Eventually, the bus was stopped at a roadblock, and in the ensuing firefight, two of the terrorists were killed. The news reports made no mention of the other two until several days later, when it was reported that they had died of wounds suffered during the firefight. A photographer who had been on the scene had snapped a picture of the two, apparently in good health, being led away by Shin Bet agents. Demands for an inquiry had met with relentless delays, until the government finally acknowledged that the two terrorists had died as a result of beatings during interrogation. Shin Bet claimed that they had been killed not during Shin Bet's interrogation, but rather while under the supervision of General Yitzhak Mordechai.

It took more than a year to reveal that in a disgraceful act of cowardice, Shin Bet had created a fraudulent frame-up of Mordechai in an attempt to cover up its own killing of the two Arab men. As if that weren't bad enough, the frame-up had been masterminded by Avraham Shalom, the head of Shin Bet. The sordid affair became public as a result of Shin Bet personnel breaking ranks to make the facts public. Needless to say, the Israeli people were devastated. It was the appearance of this front-page story in *Koteret Rashit,* that absorbed everyone's attention, and nobody had much time for an article about archaeologists who might be working for Gush Emunim.

Adam, however, was deeply distressed. He turned to a friend who had at one time been a member of his kibbutz. The friend was assistant editor at *Monitin,* a competitor of *Koteret Rashit.* For its article, *Monitin* interviewed Professor Mazar whose unconditional support for Adam confirmed the legitimacy of Adam's science and the credibility of his valuable research. Since then, I have wondered whether the *Koteret Rashit* article would have helped us or hurt us if it had not appeared during the Shin Bet scandal. Even bad publicity is sometimes preferable to silence.

My trip to New York was both personally revitalizing and also beneficial to our project. I was able to secure a commitment from a friend of mine, an investment banker. He pledged—contingent upon my receiving all the necessary approvals— to raise funds for the Ebal project. I returned to Israel with my enthusiasm refreshed, eager to continue.

Time was passing, and I was still waiting for the Regional Council to schedule a meeting for negotiations about the proposed park. I wanted to make sure that the park would generate a reasonable number of visitors, so I met with Benny Benzur, the head of one of largest tour-bus companies in Israel. Benny, himself a licensed tour guide, came to visit the site, and his reaction convinced me that my assumptions were right on target. He was so enthusiastic, he even proposed a partnership to develop the route for one-day tours of Samaria.

I had no reason to expect problems, but I was wrong. Two members of the council had been appointed to negotiate with me. In the style typical of Israeli bureaucrats, they came to me and said that before the negotiations could proceed, I needed to come up with $30,000 that would be used to preserve the site. My response was emphatic. No sane businessman, I said, would put up a nickel before there was a deal, supported by government approval for developing the site. Were they looking for charity? They had certainly come to the wrong place.

I had presented the proposal to my friend the investment banker, explaining that with some of the proceeds going for scientific development, we would be creating the possibility of additional tourist sites. There was absolutely no way that I would return to him and ask for that $30,000. This project was not to be treated as a charity. In addition, my offer to the council contained a commitment to preserve the site, a necessary prerequisite for allowing public visits.

I could see that these men were deaf to my words, so I persuaded them to meet with my lawyer, Isaac, who spent the better part of an hour trying to drum some sense through their thick bureaucratic skulls. He explained that if we were able to put the package together and proceed, the tourist site would create jobs for a good number of settlers in the immediate area. There were few employment opportunities in the West Bank. Except for those who taught in local schools or held municipal-government jobs, settlers had to commute several hours every day to their jobs in and around Tel Aviv. Isaac told the "negotiators" that in all his years as a lawyer who focused on setting up business enterprises, he had never encountered anything like their demand for the $30,000 advance. They were adamant, and they would not budge.

I turned to Benny Katzover and tried to reason with him. It was hopeless. The Shomron Regional Council, no different from any other Israeli government agency, was unable to approach a new business effort without making life miserable for entrepreneurs and investors. This case, I thought, was even worse than the norm. All we were asking was that the council agree to act as an official rubber stamp to a venture that would have generated income for the region.

Having devoted all my energies to this project, my personal financial health had deteriorated to an all-time low. I had to look for a new job. Tourism was slow, and hotels were letting people go. It took me several months to find a new position in hotel management. The job was stable, but because it was in Tiberias, 100 miles away, I had to spend every other night away from home.

Being away was not the worst part. In December 1987 the first intifada erupted, and every trip along the roads of Samaria was a terrifying adventure. Aside from dodging rocks thrown at my car as I drove home, I had to be extremely careful of piles of burning tires, heaps of trash and garbage, and clusters of bent nails that turned each road into a treacherous obstacle course. A sane driver would not dare to slow down and let his car become an easy target for huge rocks that were smashed through the windows. The army increased its presence, but their orders constrained them from having any real effect. Some of my neighbors vented their anger and frustration on the soldiers, and that did nothing to improve our public image. The settlers had come to the West Bank with government approval, and they were expected to grin and bear whatever came their way.

And don't think that it was easy to secure compensation for the damage to our cars. Most people opted to postpone the three-day ordeal of form filing until their battered cars were showing severe signs of rust and damage. Even after completing every form and standing in every line, people found that the compensation never met the actual cost of the repairs. After a while, with so much glass being shattered by the rocks of the intifada, the government introduced its solution: unbreakable plastic windows.

As I drove the route between Tiberias and Shavei Shomron, my car was the target of iron bars, metal projectiles from slingshots, and even an old refrigerator somebody hurled from the third story of a roadside house. My neighbors and I were completely frustrated. Although the country was under the Likud leadership of Yitzhak Shamir, who sympathized with us, he was one of the least powerful prime ministers in Israel's history. He feared that if he ordered the army to finish off the intifada decisively, Israel would forfeit financial support from the United States.

The Arabs were quick to pick up on Israel's hesitation to use force to stop their violence, and years later, the intifada continues to rage. The Palestinian Authority, emboldened by Israel's seeming lack of conviction, has introduced a succession of increasingly refined ways to kill Jews—mortars, grenades, sniper rifles, and, of course, suicide bombers.

As it became clearer that the Palestinians' bellicose stance was not going to change anytime soon, our plans to build the park simply fizzled. In 1990 my attention was diverted from the project when a Boston, Massachusetts-based member of my family was diagnosed with a serious illness. Trying to help and offer some comfort, I made frequent trips to Boston. Adam was taking a sabbatical at Harvard during the 1990-1991 academic year, and I enjoyed visiting with him at the apartment he had rented in Chestnut Hill, a Boston suburb. The intifada had curtailed most of Adam's fieldwork. And because it was so dangerous for Jews to drive through Nablus to get to Ebal, excavations at the site were out of the question, and the nearly completed survey also had to be neglected.

Adam's year at Harvard proved disappointing. He had expected that his hosts, the faculty of the Department of Semitic Studies, would ask him to lecture at least once. Instead, they pretty much ignored him, leaving it to the Department of Anthropology to invite him to speak about Ebal. He felt, he said, like a mathematician presenting his work before chemists, and he resented being treated like a pariah.

Still bruised from our dreadful and fruitless attempt to raise funds for Adam's research, Adam and I were amazed at the apparent ease with which Harvard faculty attract financing. At about that time, a friend told me a story about a Jewish philanthropist, who had determined to put up a million dollars to search for traces of the Hebrew patriarch Abraham. (Abraham, it turns out, was also the name of the donor's father.) To the philanthropist's mind, no institution other than Harvard could possibly achieve his goals. And his magnanimous gift fell like manna from heaven into the lap of Larry Staeger, a noted Harvard scholar. The Bible tells us that Abraham came from Mesopotamia, today's Iraq and Syria. Staeger initiated his explorations at several sites in Iraq, and when his search found nothing, he turned to Syria. Once the Syrian government learned that the project was being funded by a Jew and that the goal was to unearth signs of Abraham, Staeger was thrown out on his ear. A brief review of the potential for finding something in Israel related to Abraham also drew a blank.

At that point, Staeger urged his benefactor to reconsider his project and suggested that another biblical figure, for example, Samson, might be an acceptable subject for his investigations. Reluctantly, the man agreed, and Staeger embarked on a series of excavations at Ashkelon. Despite a lavishly provisioned expedition, Staeger did no better in his search for Samson. He did find a graveyard for dogs, which were considered sacred during the Persian period that spanned the first quarter of the seventh century CE, and a well-preserved Byzantine brothel whose beautiful mosaic designs on the walls and floor leave little to the imagination. A million dollars to unearth a canine cemetery and a whorehouse! What really stings me is the knowledge that less than 5 percent of Staeger's funding could have financed an excavation at the site Adam had identified as Elon Moreh, Abraham's first stop in the land of Israel!

In spite of the academic slights, Adam's sabbatical came as a welcome relief from his disappointments in Israel. Adam's wife, Judith, who didn't mind the 12-

month breather away from her job in the kibbutz factory, fell in love with U.S. television. Navot, Adam's youngest son, who was then 13, also found it easy to adapt to life in the United States. I was amused to see that he was sporting a trendy American hairdo complete with a small tail that hung down his neck.

On one of my visits to Boston, Adam took me with him to one of Harvard's many libraries. As we were searching for a book, a young woman who had heard us conversing in Hebrew approached us and told us that she edited the *Harvard Theological Review,* one of the most prestigious journals in the field. Never one to miss an opportunity, I told her about the excavation at Ebal, including my own belief that the site had been a temple. Suggesting that I write an article for the journal, she gave me a copy of its guidelines for submissions. I did eventually send her an article, but I found the word-count constraints made it impossible for me to present a convincing case, and the article was not accepted for publication. To prove that the existence of the site ought to affect the dating of Deuteronomy, I would have had to examine all the existing theories on the subject and deal with them one by one. I had neither the time nor the resources.

I had been making an effort to develop business opportunities during each of my trips to Boston. Of course, none of my initiatives did more than fizzle. Had I not been so consumed by the conundrums of biblical archaeology, one of my schemes might have panned out.

I had none of the academic credentials I'd need to pursue biblical research at any university, and the intifada had destroyed our hopes for developing the site for tourism. Furthermore, my personal circumstances had deteriorated to an all-time low. I had declined into a state of depression that made life so unbearable for everyone that my wife and I eventually divorced. The separation from my wife and children was excruciatingly painful, and after enduring the most remarkably unproductive period of my life, I decided that if I ever wanted to recover, I would have to move myself far away from Ebal, my curse. That it was also a blessing was difficult to grasp during those difficult days.

So it was with enormous anguish that I made the decision to stay in the United States where I would try to sort myself out. I did not know whether I would ever be able to recover, but I knew that if I remained in Israel, I would destroy not only myself but my family as well. I could not allow everyone to endure the pain that was consuming me.

As if I were haunted by a Dybbuk, an evil Jewish spirit, my soul was possessed by an obsession with Ebal. I was compelled to pursue my ideas until I could convince myself that there was nothing more I could do. Over the course of the next decade, I would, from time to time, sit down and write the record of these thoughts. I was convinced that eventually, I would be able to share my story with the world.

Finally, I have reached that point.

Deuteronomy

This day you have become a nation to the Lord
your God. (Deuteronomy 27:9.)

When did the loose association of Israelite tribes coalesce into one nation?

That question has been the focus of considerable discussion and scholarly controversy. Most biblical scholars agree that by the time of King David, around 1000 BCE, the tribes had blended and become a single nation, but beyond that, opinions diverge. I contend that Israel's first assertion of national identity occurred neither at Sinai nor in Jerusalem, but at Mount Ebal. Except for the above sentence—an excerpt from Moses' recitation of the commandments related to the ceremony of the blessings and the curses—the Bible says nothing about an act of national unification. That ceremony—one of the series of biblical covenants between God and Israel—sets the stage for the Israelites' declaration of nationhood. This observation is, of course, directly related to Ebal's having been the site of the First Temple of Israel.

It is my blessing to have made this observation. And it has been my curse that my conclusions about Ebal are so incompatible with both the traditional and the scientific understanding of the Bible that neither the religious nor the scholarly community has responded with any level of interest. The lessons I learned from Ebal have shattered the religious beliefs with which I grew up, destroying my relationship with the traditional religious community. Turning to members of the scientific establishment, I have met with rock-solid resistance to revisiting established thinking.

One day about 13 years ago, my wife and I went to Tel Aviv's Dizengoff Center—an indoor shopping mall—to see a movie. After the film, we stopped at a café, and as we were sipping our coffee, I looked up and saw Menahem Michelson and his wife walking toward us. I had known Menahem for years. We had first met at Bar Ilan University, where we had worked together on the student newspaper. In more recent years, our paths had rarely crossed, so I was pleased to see him. Menahem had pursued a career in journalism, and over the years, he had made his way up the professional ladder at one of Israel's most popular daily newspapers. What an opportunity, I thought. Here was a person who might be willing to help me publicize our story. I invited Menahem and his wife to join us, and, after the usual pleasantries, I launched into the story of the excavations at Mount Ebal.

Menahem was attentive, but I could see that he was listening with mounting skepticism. Clearly it was only because of our longstanding friendship that he was making any effort at all to mask his incredulity. When I concluded my narration, he asked only, "Which *gadol,* (Hebrew for a great scholar of Judaica) agrees with you?" His response was completely reasonable, but it made me want to laugh. I had, in fact, taken one gadol to view the site, and his response had been both unexpectedly candid and disappointingly honest.

That gadol, a renowned rabbi and scholar of Talmud, taught in Jerusalem and had spent many years lecturing in a U.S. university as well. I had showed him every aspect of the site, carefully presenting details I wouldn't show to a less educated person. Throughout my monologue he was quiet, interrupting only to ask a few highly specific questions. When I reached the end of my presentation, I looked him in the eye and asked his opinion. Taking a deep breath, he said, "I am sorry to say that I have to agree with your conclusions. However, if I live a thousand years, I will never admit that out loud."

A respected rabbinic figure could not be expected to agree with conclusions that undermine the roots of rabbinic Judaism no matter how well founded those conclusions might be. And, hearing Menahem's question, I realized that it would be pointless to continue that discussion. For him, a religious journalist, any biblical concept that is in conflict with rabbinic opinion cannot be valid.

With precious few exceptions, my experiences with academic scholars also have proved fruitless.

For more than a decade, I have been searching for scholarly references that support Ebal's being the chosen place. I have to admit that not even Adam is willing to define Ebal as a temple, so I knew that I'd be unlikely to find support from other scholars. I have read a number of articles and books that imply that Ebal might have been the site of an altar, but the widely accepted scholarly identification of Deuteronomy with the Josiah episode was outweighing any other considerations. When I had nearly given up all hope, however, I found precisely what I had been looking for.

On one of my many visits to New York City, I visited the library of Hebrew Union College in Greenwich Village and came across a doctoral dissertation by a G.A. Danell, from Upsala University in Stockholm. Published in 1946, one year before my birth, Danell's thesis, "Studies in the Name Israel in the Old Testament," examines the use of the name "Israel" in each and every book of the Old Testament. Danell explains that Israel was used with five distinct meanings. It is used as the name God gave to the patriarch Jacob, the name of the land, the name of the entire nation, the name of the northern kingdom of ten tribes that seceded during the reign of Solomon's son Rehoboam, and the name of the kingdom of Judah on one occasion, after the ten tribes had "disappeared."

Danell's chapter on Deuteronomy astonished me. Working through Deuteronomy sentence by sentence, paragraph by paragraph, Danell had come to conclusions that match mine almost exactly. And he had formed his opinions never having seen—or even dreamt about—the physical evidence that, at the time of his writing, was still buried at Ebal.

At this point, I must beg the reader's forbearance. Up to now, I have done all I can to avoid burdening you with endless texts quoted from the academic presses of the world. After all, this is not a textbook, and I'd rather not deaden your enthusiasm with soporific citations. In this case, however, I am obliged to make an exception, if only to let you see for yourself the remarkable similarity of my conclusions to what Danell says about Deuteronomy.

> But would it not be a much more natural assumption that the present position of the Shechem [Ebal] passages in Dt [the major source of Deuteronomy] is original? Since the rest of Dt, as we have tried to show above, has a number of northern Israelite traits, it is most natural to assume that the similar northern Israelite passages, 11:26

and following and chapter 27, also belong to the original body. If these passages are really meant to identify Shechem with "the Place that Yahweh chooses," it seems reasonable to assume that this is also the original purpose of the book, and that its application to Jerusalem is a later interpretation rather than that a later reviser should have tried to put Shechem instead of Jerusalem. When and how could such a manipulation ever really have been possible?

The present composition is in my opinion by no means so impossible as is usually thought. The construction of the book may be compared to a medieval altar-piece, where the corpus corresponds to the codex proper, 12-26, while the inner wings correspond to the two Ebal-Gerizim passages, 11:26 and chapter 27, and the outer wings to the historical and parenthetic passages that introduce and close the book. Even if it is not directly stated that Ebal is "the Place which Yahweh chooses," there are quite clear indications of it. The altar to be built to Yahweh on Ebal in 27:5, must be the altar at Yahweh's chosen place, mentioned in 26:4 and implied in 12:5 and following. The sacrifice is described in 27:6 and in 12:6 in very similar terms.

It is easier to conceive that the original place of Shechem in Dt has been somewhat dimmed by direct references to this place being removed by Jerusalemite revision, than that Jerusalem has been removed by an interpolation dictated by ecclesiastical policy. That the Shechem passages have been added only out of piety to an old tradition, is on the other hand hardly probable. The purpose must have been something more than traditionalism for its own sake.

Thirty-six years before our shovels had broken ground at Ebal, Danell had reached conclusions that matched ideas I had developed as I worked at and studied Ebal for more than a decade. Of course, my luck being what it is, I didn't come across

Danell's book until several months after receiving final notification that my paper would not be accepted for publication in the *Harvard Theological Review*. In any case, I don't know how much difference Danell's support would have made. I showed his dissertation to a widely respected scholar, and he, echoing Menahem's reaction, told me that if Danell's assessment "had been written by a gadol, such as Albrecht Alt or Martin Noth, I would have no problem accepting it." And the world of biblical scholarship is not so different from the world of the traditional rabbis: whatever does not jibe with accepted theory may be discarded almost a priori. Only a gadol can overcome the institutionalized barriers. It doesn't matter that my evidence is correct and that there are no arguments that seriously challenge my contentions. Religious experts and university scholars—each of them rejected my conclusions out of hand, asking me implicitly and explicitly, "Who are you to make these assumptions?"

I have never considered myself a "scholar" as the word is commonly understood. Nevertheless, you should know that I began studying biblical and Jewish texts at the tender age of three. As I've matured intellectually and grown older, the breadth and depth of my studies also has expanded, and over the years, I have read all that there is to read on the origins of the Bible, delving deeply into and returning to many of these texts time and again.

Hebrew University Professor Yehezkel Kaufmann, one of the greatest biblical scholars of the 20th century, was the author of a monumental six-volume opus, *Toldot Ha'emunah HaYisraelit*, or "Origins of the Israelite Faith." Abridged and translated, the work was published in English under the title, *The Religion of Israel*. Only a few extremely dedicated scholars have bothered to study the exceedingly detailed original version. Nevertheless, because of my enormous interest in the material Kaufmann covered in that work, since 1981 I have read and reread the original six volumes—4,000 pages—a half-dozen times.

Whereas Wellhausen, the German biblical scholar, maintained that P, the priestly source, was very late, dating only to the Second Temple period, Kaufmann says that P, originated in the earliest stages of the Israelite faith. It's important to note the huge implications of their disagreement, which reflects on the historical legitimacy of the religion of Israel, as well as its nationhood. According to Wellhausen, the cultic history of Israel was a product of the latter part of the first millennium BCE, and therefore Christianity should be recognized as the monotheistic "successor" to the Israelite religion.

Kaufmann set out to prove Wellhausen wrong, and except on one point, he was quite successful. Unable to prove otherwise, Kaufmann was forced to acknowledge the strength of the argument that dates the D source to the time of Josiah. Kauffman died in 1963, 20 years before Ebal started to reveal its long-buried secrets. If he were still alive, however, I believe that Kaufmann might have realized his struggle to provide historical validation of Israel's ancient history. What we have learned from the excavations at Mount Ebal would have complemented his remarkable scholarship, allowing him to achieve the perfection for which he had labored all his life.

Once I realized the enormous implications of my research, I had to satisfy myself that there was no chink in the armor. I was certain then, more than a decade ago, that I was right. But for my claims to have an effect, I had to be certain that my conclusions would withstand expert scrutiny. I wanted to test them in an academic context. I had met with numerous scholars individually. Some had been very helpful, some less helpful, and most had offered nothing. I made an appointment with Dr. Steven Garfunkel, then head of graduate studies at the Jewish Theological Seminary. He was very receptive and suggested I contact Dr. Mary Callaway a lecturer at Fordham College. Callaway coordinated a monthly lecture series at Columbia University for college professors. It took several attempts, but I finally managed to contact her and arrange a meeting. After hearing my story, she agreed to give me an opportunity to present my findings to this distinguished forum. She was quite encouraging, saying that it would be refreshing to hear from someone like me, who comes from outside the cloisters of biblical scholarship—somebody who had actually muddied his boots in an excavation.

True to her word, Callaway scheduled the lecture, and December 16, 1992, found me in the unusual situation of being dressed in a suit and tie. She had invited me to join her and the seminar participants for dinner at the Faculty Club before the presentation. I had no appetite, so I occupied myself in observing my dinner companions. Everyone was friendly and polite, but it was easy to sense the competitive undercurrents that circulated very close to the surface. Just as I had idealized rabbis when I was observant and Orthodox, I had expected the professors to be above petty rivalries and back biting. I continually have to remind myself that for all their knowledge and their exalted positions, even the most highly regarded professors are, after all, people like the rest of us.

After dinner, we adjourned to a small room with a long rectangular table. A total of 15 people were attending, and a number of them had skipped the dinner and headed directly to the lecture room. I had brought slides to complement my lecture, and although the slide projector was faulty, requiring me to insert each slide manually, the presentation went very well. I had been told that I should speak for 40 to 45 minutes, leaving 10 to 15 minutes for a question-and-answer period.

Each of the 15 had an extensive and intensive background in biblical studies. As experts in Bible and ancient Middle Eastern studies, they already were quite familiar with the accepted views on Deuteronomy. I introduced my remarks by saying that I wanted the group to perform the role of devil's advocate, and I looked forward to their attacking my ideas from every conceivable angle. I had no academic ax to grind, I said, and my aim in making the presentation was to test my theory against their expertise. Please, I said, feel free to attack, no holds barred.

And attack they did. They barraged me with questions and challenges that continued not for 10 to 15 minutes as planned, but for more than two hours. Nevertheless, I was able to respond intelligently to each question, and nobody presented an argument that refuted my assumptions. I had the peculiar feeling that perhaps I was dreaming. Whenever there was a lull in the questioning, I begged for more. Finally, when there were no more questions, the session ended, and as I was returning my slides to their box, one of the men approached me and said, "You know, you may be right. What we really know about Deuteronomy doesn't amount to very much, and there is more guesswork there than we'd like to admit."

If I had been pursuing the academic path, I should have published an article in one of the scholarly biblical-studies journals. I did submit a paper to a journal in the New York City area, but it was not accepted. I admit that I did not do justice to the vastness of the topic. It's simply impossible to prove my point—that not only is the altar at Ebal a temple, but that it was the first Temple—in 40 pages. A thorough treatment would require reviewing a huge corpus of biblical scholarship, and I will never have the time, money, or access to adequate research facilities to develop the monograph my topic warrants. Furthermore, I know I lack the right connections and credentials. I was gratified that the journal's editor had made some positive comments about my paper, but I still cannot understand the editor's reasoning for rejecting it for publication. When I mentioned my bewilderment to a man who was the head of the Bible department at a prestigious research institution, he laughed and started to recite the lengthy list of his articles that had been rejected for publication, despite his own very impressive credentials.

As I mentioned earlier in this book, I no longer feel bound to any recognized stream of Jewish observance—not Orthodox, Conservative, Reform, or Reconstructionist. Paradoxically, however, my identity as a Jew—a descendant of the people who wrote the Bible—grows stronger with every moment I devote to my biblical investigations. My identity with the land of Israel, as well as the nation of Israel, has intensified, and from this point of view, I have to say that the future looks bleak indeed.

As a result of U.S. pressure, one Israeli government after another has been forced to deal gingerly with the Arab intifada and "negotiate" with Yasser Arafat. I find it absolutely incredible that a few dozen stone-throwing Arab children, the primary force of the first intifada, have brought Israel—a country that had defeated the armies of its powerful Arab neighbors time and time again—to its knees.

When Israeli representatives first met with the Palestinian delegation in Oslo, they discovered that the chief concern of the Palestinians was not their economic plight, which after all is a direct result of the intifada's disruption of economic life in the West Bank and Gaza. Nor were they set on gaining political concessions— being allowed to hold free elections or gaining control of such public functions as education and health care. In fact, what they wanted—above all else—was control of West Bank's archaeological sites.

The Israeli negotiators were surprised by what seemed to them to be an innocuous demand. I, however, was horrified, and I have to admit that I was amazed that the Palestinians—more than Israelis themselves—had realized what it is that really makes Israel tick. Israel's archaeology is the strongest link between the nation of Israel and the land of Israel. In Israel, where religious observance is spotty and the subject of heated contention, the significant archaeological sites— especially those in the West Bank—are the glue that connects Israelis with their history and tradition, and to one another. Breaking that connection would reinforce the Arabs' longstanding claim: rather than a nation, Israel is a religion, and consequently, Israel does not deserve a state.

I dread a future in which self-governing Palestinians have jurisdiction over Mount Ebal, the site of Israel's birth as a nation. Giving up the West Bank could mean the end of Israel's statehood, which has been revived only briefly after a 2,000-year lapse. For me this is beyond consideration.

Would the U.S. government, in a moment of clouded thinking, return Manhattan to the Indians who had been tricked into selling their native lands to European newcomers? Absurd, you say. And I say, Israel's ceding control of the West Bank is even more absurd than the possibility of handing over any U.S. city to Native Americans. Ebal, says the Bible, is the place, the site of Israel's First Temple, the site that inspired Israel's creation as a nation. And the Bible, the best-selling book of all time, has been the source of inspiration for 2,000 years of Western civilization. Regretfully, I admit that I do not have answers to the political problems that Israel faces today. I hope only that as the politicians struggle to find solutions, they will be mindful of the Gordian knot of historical awareness that, more than anything else, makes Israel a nation.

In the same way, the book of Deuteronomy has been at the core of my research efforts and continues to inform my vision of my personal future: *[11]For this commandment that I command you today—it is not hidden from you and it is not distant. [12]It is not in heaven, [for you] to say, "Who can ascend to the heaven for us and take it for us, so that we can listen to it and perform it?" [13]Nor is it across the sea, [for you] to say, "Who can cross to the other side of the sea for us and take it for us, so that we can listen to it and perform it?" [14]Rather, the matter is very near to you—in your mouth and your heart—to perform it.* (Deuteronomy 30:11-14.)

I no longer look to the heavens for inspiration, and looking for "the word" from across the sea, that is, from U.S. academe, is beyond me as well. But by writing this book, I believe I am following the instructions of the above verses: I have placed my heart—all my experiences and thoughts on the subject of Ebal—into my mouth, and I have rid myself of the demon that gave me the most uplifting of my life's blessings, as well as the most abominable of my life's curses.

As I write these words, my thoughts drift back to one day at the excavation. Adam and I were strolling down the steep path that leads from the peak of Mount Ebal to the site. He turned to me, and gesturing toward our dig, he exclaimed, "Look at that puny, primitive construction. During the period that was built, both in Mesopotamia and in Egypt, magnificent structures were being erected for cultic purposes. And our ancestors could come up with nothing better than primitive walls, primitive pottery, and a primitive altar."

I had never even considered the physical nature of the site. To me, grandeur, with or without gold, silver, and precious stones, was irrelevant. From the moment I realized that the site contained an altar, I had been struck by the realization that, unlike the cultic sites of Mesopotamia and Egypt, the temple at Ebal was situated so that all the people, whoever was in the area, would be able to see exactly what was going on at the altar. This was not a culture that had secrets, hidden rites, or a class structure that precluded participation. Cultic activities were not hidden in a heaven, nor were they beyond a vast sea.

Quoting from the prophet Zachariah, I responded to Adam saying, *This is the word of the Lord to Zerubabel: Not through armed might and not through strength, but through My spirit, said the Lord, Master of Legions.* (Zachariah 4:6.) Only the spirit endures forever. The mighty Egypt of the Pharaohs, the great powers of Babylonia, Assyria, Persia, Greece, and Rome have crumbled to dust. Israel, which against all odds has retained its spirit, has managed to survive and even rebuild a national state. Israel as a nation has lived to breathe new life into Hebrew, which for 2,000 years was familiar only to the most pious Jews and a handful of scholars.

For Israel to endure, it must retain the intangible spirit as described by Zachariah. And that spirit is nourished by a unique relationship that unites the people, the land, and the Bible of Israel. The ethnic composition of the Israeli population is continually in flux, reflecting the continuous immigration of Jews from around the world. The Bible, too, is a document with myriad interpretations. But the land—where our story begins—is constant and eternal.

Although it is my fierce prayer that I will never need a Palestinian visa to visit that land, I hope that my love of and my rights to that land will never infringe on the rights of any other people. How will we manage that? I leave that to the politicians. How do I cherish and sustain what I have learned from Ebal? It's up to me to let those lessons shed clarifying light on all the days of my life.

The Scarab

*The scarab pictured here is from the archaeological site at Mount Ebal, in Israel.
See description on next page.*

Appendix

The scarab was the seal of ancient Egypt. Every scarab is shaped like a beetle, has beetle-like sculpted markings upon its rounded upper surface, and a series of symbols carved on the flat bottom.

The scarab pictured here is from the archaeological site at Mount Ebal, in Israel.

Near the upper edge there is a salamander, which means "many." To its right, a crouching archer holds a double bow. The Egyptian symbol for a galley boat, powered by many slaves, appears near the bottom.

The figure at the left, enclosed in an oblong line is called a "cartouche," or sign of the king. Archaelogical experts have identified this cartouche as having belonged to Ramses II (1290-1226BCE), whom most agree was the Pharoah of the Exodus.

The scarab tells us:

"Ramses II is a great king because he has many archers and boats."

To date, three scarabs identical to this one have been discovered: two in Egypt and one in Cyprus. All three of those were unearthed in places known to have been built by Ramses II. The site at Ebal reveals absolutely no signs of Egyptian design: there is no doubt about the site's Israelite origins.

There is only one way this scarab could have made its way to Mount Ebal where archaeologists found it after 3,000 years. Someone had to have taken it from the court of Pharoah, carried it through the Sinai Desert, and deliberately buried it at this first Israelite Temple in the land of Israel.

This scarab is quite possibly our first extra-Biblical evidence of Exodus.

Remarkable Similarity

The diagram is an archaeological artist's rendering of the altar whose remains we discovered at the Mount Ebal excavation site. The drawing is very much like the sketch Adam Zertal handed me in October 1983, and is based on our archaeological findings at Mount Ebal. Note the remarkable similarity of the archaeologist's drawing to the picture on the right—the Mishnaic rendition of the altar that was in the second Temple in Jerusalem.

L RIT-MEYER

Before and After

The photo on the top of this page shows the site as it was when Adam and the survey crew first visited it in April, 1980. At the time, the site's only distinguishing feature was its rich abundance of pottery shards.

The photo below was taken after five seasons of excavation. The altar was found after removing the huge pile of stones shown above. Note the double ramp; one leads to the top and the other leads to a mid-level ramp that provided access to all corners of the altar.